by Rachel Carley

Illustrations by
Ray Skibinski
and Ed Lam

A ROUNDTABLE PRESS BOOK

AN OWL BOOK

Henry Holt and Company / New York

The Visual

Dictionary of

American

Domestic

Architecture

Henry Holt and Company, LLC
Publishers since 1866
115 West 18th Street
New York, New York 10011

Henry Holt® is a registered trademark
of Henry Holt and Company, LLC.

Library of Congress Cataloging-in-Publication Data
Carley, Rachel.
The visual dictionary of American domestic architecture /
Rachel Carley; illustrated by Ray Skibinski.—1st ed.
p. cm.
Includes index.
ISBN 0-8050-4563-5 (An Owl Book: pbk)
1. Architecture, Domestic—United States—Dictionaries.
2. Architecture—United States—Dictionaries. I. Title.
NA7205.C27   1994   94-20071
728'.0973—dc20   CIP

Henry Holt books are available for special promotions and
premiums. For details contact: Director, Special Markets.

First published in hardcover in 1994
by Henry Holt Reference Books

First Owl Books Edition 1997

Designed by Betty Binns

A Roundtable Press Book

Printed in the United States of America

10 9 8

Contents

Acknowledgments

Each of the more than 500 labeled illustrations in *The Visual Dictionary of American Domestic Architecture* was drawn specifically for this volume. Gathering the research materials on which these pictures were based was an extensive undertaking, and it would not have been possible without the generosity and help of numerous individuals, libraries, museums, and preservation organizations across the country.

I am grateful for the advice and expertise shared by Andrew Scott Dolkart of the Columbia University School of Architecture. I also thank the following: the staff of the American Indian Archaeological Institute in Washington, Connecticut, and the Museum of the American Indian in New York City; Jonathan Fricker, Director of the Division of Historic Preservation, Baton Rouge; the staff of the Missouri Historical Society; Phoebe Hopkins of the Berks County Conservancy in Pennsylvania; the library staff of the Museum of New Mexico in Santa Fe; and Hope and Kenneth LeVan of Oley, Pennsylvania, who gave me a memorable tour of early Germanic buildings in that state and provided measured drawings of their own home.

The periodical and rare book collections of Avery Architectural Library at Columbia University were an invaluable resource for this project. I am also grateful to the library and archives of the American Institute of Architects in Washington, D.C., which houses the George P. Lindsay Collection published in the White Pine Monograph Series. (Many of these monographs have been reprinted in a multi-volume series, *The Architectural Treasures of Early America*, published by the National Historical Society of Harrisburg, Pennsylvania.)

I am indebted to the scholarship of numerous architectural historians whose original research and published work were of great help: Abbott Lowell Cummings for his work on the postmedieval architecture of colonial Massachussetts; Andrew Scott Dolkart for his research on the Greek Revival; Robert Easton and Peter Nabokov for their extensive study of Native American architecture; Ronald Haase for his documentation of the Cracker architecture of Florida; Thomas Hubka for his theory on the connected farm buildings of Maine; Sarah Landau for her theory on the origins of the Stick Style; Albert Manucy for his research on the early architecture of St. Augustine, Florida; William McMillen for his research on early Dutch and English Colonial building technology; Charles Peterson for his documentation of the French houses of the Illinois Country; Robert St. George and Robert F. Trent for their research and fieldwork in 17th-century New England building; John Michael Vlach for his study on the origins of the shotgun house; and William Woys Weaver for his research on early Germanic buildings in Pennsylvania.

Finally, I extend my sincere thanks to Marsha Melnick, Susan Meyer, and the entire staff of Roundtable Press, and especially to Ray Skibinski and Ed Lam, two talented and remarkably patient illustrators, who often did double duty as architects.

Introduction

When I was approached with the idea of a dictionary of American architecture, my first reaction was, "How do you *define* architecture?" There is, of course, an accepted vocabulary of terms for the various elements of a building, but by breaking anything down into individual parts out of context, you risk obscuring the broader picture. With these concerns in mind, *The Visual Dictionary of American Domestic Architecture* evolved as an illustrated reference guide to American building that defines terminology through the universal language of pictures, but also attempts to explain architectural types and styles within the framework of the social, historical, geographic, climactic, and ethnic influences that shaped them.

To help narrow down the subject, this book is concerned exclusively with domestic building, which answered its own distinctive needs and purposes independent of civic, religious, and commercial architecture. Beginning with the indigenous dwelling types of Native American groups and working up to the 1990s, styles and types are presented chronologically, grouped by chapters according to the names and periods by which they are generally recognized.

In reality, of course, buildings don't fall so neatly into categories, and what emerges is a fascinating timeline of both continuity and contrasts. From the beginning of European settlement until the post-Revolutionary period, the prevailing tastes in American architectural styles—which were extremely fashion-conscious—closely mirrored changing trends in England, albeit 20 years or so behind. That, however, is only part of the picture. Isolated by politics, religion, and language, many settlements, such as those established by the French in the Mississippi Valley and by the Spanish in Florida and the Southwest, had their own distinctly individual character. These colonies may have been on the same continent as colonies founded contemporaneously by English, Dutch, and Germanic immigrants, but for all intents and purposes they were foreign countries to one another.

As communication and transportation improved, and as territories changed hands, building styles and traditions were absorbed to some degree from one culture to another. From the start, however, while one thing was happening, something else was always going on. Currents in architecture overlapped, incorporating features from one style that was going out with those of another style coming in. Moreover, the houses built by one economic class were entirely different from those of another. This was as true in the 1600s as it was in the Victorian era, when it was just as common to spend thousands of dollars on imported marble as it was to order gingerbread trim from a catalog—and it remains true today.

In an effort to present a comprehensive picture of changing currents and trends, *The Visual Dictionary of American Domestic Architecture* illustrates both high-style and vernacular buildings, exploring urban, rural, and regional variations. Each chapter not only offers several exterior views, but also tries to present the many elements that are integral to defining and identifying a particular style or type, including floor plans, interior architectural features, and characteristic details, as well as barns, garages, and other outbuildings. Also included throughout the volume are diagrams that explain the underpinnings or "anatomy" of building structures. Among these anatomies are structural systems distinctive to a particular group, such as the anchorbent frame of the Dutch colonists, along with innovations such as the balloon frame, which precipitated major changes in the development of American architecture.

The idea behind this multilayered approach is that it is not enough to show *what* something looked like: This visual dictionary seeks to put enough pieces together to explain *why* it looked that way. In order not to repeat what has already been accomplished by other architectural reference books, I have made an effort to present buildings and elements that are representative of their period but have not been published frequently before.

The majority of the illustrations are based on designs and advertisements published in contemporary journals. Many of the Victorian buildings, for example, come from the pages of *American Architect and Building News*, begun in 1876 as the first magazine in America devoted to architectural design. Others derive from popular plan books of the late 19th and early 20th centuries. Still others are based on the photographs and measured drawings of the Historic American Buildings Survey (HABS), a government-sponsored program that has documented thousands of historic buildings since 1933 (many now demolished). This kind of research has made it possible to show a single element in great detail, such as both sides of the same door, and it has yielded many surprises, ranging from the startling graphic interior paint patterns used by German Colonial settlers to a garage designed in 1916 as a miniature Swiss chalet.

The Visual Dictionary of American Domestic Architecture is designed to be both a reference book and a field guide, intended for students, architects, and anybody curious about the buildings they see in their own neighborhoods. No single book can offer a definitive analysis of a subject as complex as American architecture, but I hope that through simple labeled illustrations, this dictionary will answer questions, clarify terms, and invite readers to explore. In the end, there is no better way to learn about buildings than to look at them.

The Visual Dictionary of American Domestic Architecture

Chapter One
Native American Dwellings

At the time of European colonization in the 16th and 17th centuries, there were some 300 native groups in North America. While Native American shelters differed significantly across the continent, three broad types can be identified: pole- and sapling-framed dwellings, more substantial gable-roofed timber and plank houses, and "earth" homes made primarily of mud, clay, or stone. Many of these indigenous building types date back thousands of years; some are still used today.

Quite naturally, Native American building evolved in direct response to climate, local materials, and hunting and farming patterns, as well as to social and religious organization. Wood structures prevailed in the forested areas of the East, the Great Lakes, California, and the Northwest Coast. Peoples of the Southwest and lower Mississippi recognized the advantage of mud plaster made from local clay or adobe (sun-dried earth and straw), which absorbs heat during the day and holds it in at night. In the Deep South, cool open-air shelters developed, raised off the ground to provide protection from snakes and flooding. All groups adapted their homes to changing seasons, using shade arbors in hot weather, and erecting windbreaks of planks, thatch, or adobe and adding warm interior liners for winter months.

On the Great Plains, the portable hide-covered tipi served the seminomadic buffalo-hunting tribes, who used dogs, and later horses, to transport the dismantled framing poles to new hunting grounds. Painted tipi patterns held mystical meanings, which might also affect the siting of a dwelling. The Plains Indians, for example, revered the circle as a symbol of the nest, and the Navajo hogan always faces east, toward the rising sun.

Pole and Sapling Frame

ALGONQUIAN WIGWAM
(NORTHEAST AND GREAT LAKES)

BARK TIE DETAIL

FRAME

stringers
bark tie
bent sapling
fire ring

reed mat
bark
saplings

smoke hole
sapling tie-down
reed mat covering (birch, elm, cedar, and chestnut bark also used)
window opening
fire ring
sleeping pallet

Pole and Sapling Frame

IROQUOIS LONGHOUSE
(NORTHEAST AND GREAT LAKES)

smoke hole   bark covering (reed matting also used)

beam

tanned-hide door hanging

bent sapling rafter

storage platform

sleeping platforms

thatched partitions
(separate family areas)

Most Native Americans lived communally, as shown in this 16th-century
engraving after a 1585 drawing by John White. The Algonquian village of
Pomeiooc, in what is now North Carolina, consisted of barrel-roofed structures ranging from forty to one hundred feet long, and each housing several
families. Reed mat coverings could be rolled up or removed for ventilation.
During hunting and fishing seasons, the Algonquians traveled away from
their villages, setting up camp with smaller, temporary wigwams.

Pole and Sapling Frame

OJIBWA BARK HOUSE (GREAT LAKES)

ridge pole

log weight

bark covering

exterior framing poles

UMATILLA MAT HOUSE (PLATEAU REGION)

tule or cattail matting

exterior bracing poles

vertical support post

YOKUTS MAT HOUSE (SOUTHERN CALIFORNIA)

ridge pole

forked pole support

grass or tule matting

exterior bracing poles

Pole and Sapling Frame

pine poles

MAIDU HO-BE
(CALIFORNIA SIERRA NEVADA)

incense pine,
cedar, or redwood
bark slab

entrance roof

APACHE WIKIUP
(SOUTHWEST)

reed thatch

sapling tie-down

thatched sun shelter
(*ramada*)

crotched support pole

support posts
(positioned in
cardinal directions)

stringer (pecan, elm,
or hemlock)

THATCH DETAIL

prairie-grass thatch

stringer

grass sheath

WICHITA GRASS HOUSE
(GREAT PLAINS)

Pole and Sapling Frame

TIPI (GREAT PLAINS AND SOUTHWEST)

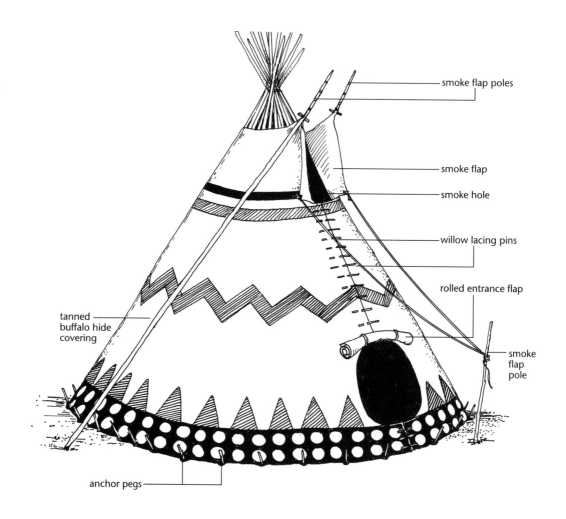

smoke flap poles

smoke flap

smoke hole

willow lacing pins

rolled entrance flap

tanned buffalo hide covering

smoke flap pole

anchor pegs

Anatomy of a Tipi

The tipi was the portable shelter of the Plains Indians, including the Cree, Blackfeet, Crow, and Cheyenne. This tentlike dwelling consisted of a basic frame of either three or four poles (of red cedar or lodgepole pine) that were positioned in cardinal directions and tilted to brace against prevailing winds, producing an oval, rather than a round, plan. Intermediate poles were laid over the frame, followed by a hide covering. When it was time to move to a new hunting ground, the disassembled parts were packed onto a drag, or travois, pulled by dogs. After horses were introduced to North America by the Spanish in the 1500s, tipis doubled in size, as these animals could pull a heavier load.

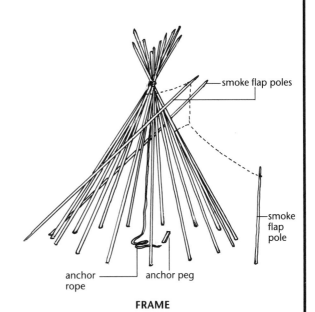

smoke flap poles

smoke flap pole

anchor rope

anchor peg

FRAME

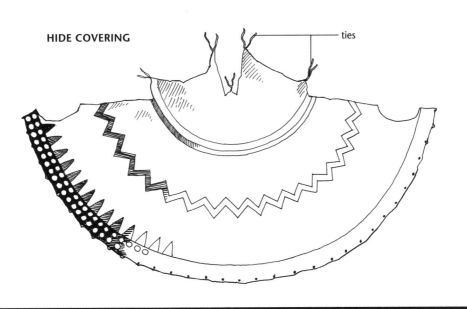

HIDE COVERING

ties

Gable Roof

SEMINOLE CHICKEE (FLORIDA)

ridge pole

stringer

rafter poles

crosstie

crossed-pole thatch weights

palmetto thatch

half-log platform (palmetto, palm, or cypress)

stilt

WATTLE-AND-DAUB HOUSE (SOUTHEAST)

stringers

rafter

king post

vertical support pole (dug into trench)

wattle (woven rods and twigs)

smoke hole

gable

cane thatch (matting also used)

mud plaster (daub)

crossed rafters

log roofing

gable

cypress or pine log siding

saddle notch

CHEROKEE LOG CABIN (SOUTHEAST)

mud chinking

OJIBWA PLANK HOUSE (GREAT LAKES)

ridge pole

extended rafter pole

gable

bark roofing

vertical plank siding

bracing pole

vertical plank door

YUROK PLANK HOUSE (NORTHERN CALIFORNIA)

extended rafter poles (willow or hazel)

round entry hole

split-plank redwood siding

gable

plate beam

wall poles

threshold boulders

TLINGIT PLANK HOUSE (ALASKA)

gable

bear iconography

softwood plank siding over cedar log frame

vertical plank door

Earth Wall

**MANDAN EARTH LODGE
(GREAT PLAINS)**

center post (four used)

willow stick   roof pole

stringer

mud plaster

fire ring   sunken floor

crotched support
post (twelve used)

smoke hole

mud plaster

entrance roof

**THOMPSON PIT HOUSE
(NORTHWESTERN PLATEAU)**

stringer

crotched
support post

notched log ladder
(tilted to east)

smoke hole

pine needle, grass,
and earth covering

excavated pit (three
to four feet deep)

stone fireplace slab
(to protect ladder)

Earth Wall

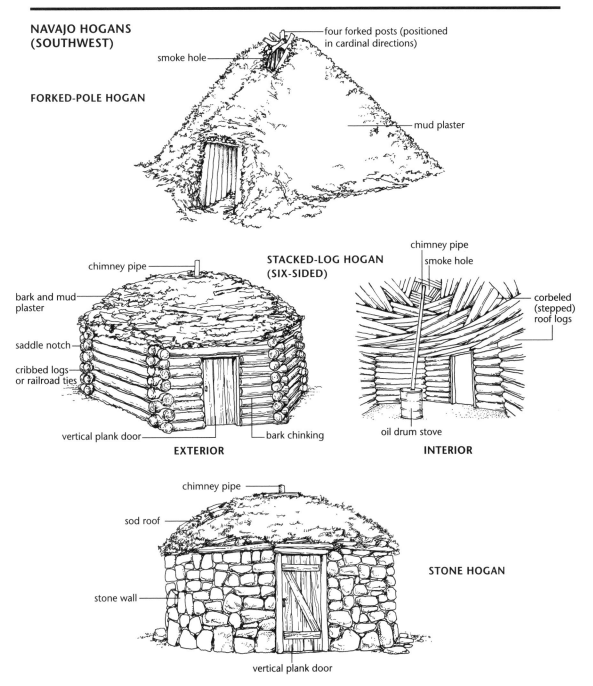

NAVAJO HOGANS
(SOUTHWEST)

four forked posts (positioned in cardinal directions)

smoke hole

FORKED-POLE HOGAN

mud plaster

chimney pipe

STACKED-LOG HOGAN
(SIX-SIDED)

chimney pipe

smoke hole

bark and mud plaster

corbeled (stepped) roof logs

saddle notch

cribbed logs or railroad ties

vertical plank door

bark chinking

oil drum stove

EXTERIOR

INTERIOR

chimney pipe

sod roof

STONE HOGAN

stone wall

vertical plank door

Earth Wall

PAPAGO MUD HOUSE (SOUTHWEST)

mesquite sun shelter *(ramada)*

crotched support pole

adobe plaster over ocotillo cactus stalks

YUMAN SAND-ROOFED HOUSE (COLORADO RIVER)

exterior framing pole   sand over earth

packed arrowwood

MOHAVE MUD HOUSE (JACAL) (COLORADO RIVER)

brush covering

adobe plaster over thatch

horizontal plank door

PUEBLO HOUSE (SOUTHWEST)

individual family units

chimney pot

roof of dry earth, packed grass, and adobe over small roof poles (latillas)

adobe plaster over mud-packed adobe brick

air vent

rainspout (canale)

beam (viga)

plaza

beams (vigas)

roof poles (latillas)

crotched support post

bench (banco)   whitewashed plaster

fireplace (fogón)

Chapter Two
Continental Influences

The first Europeans to establish a strong identity in America were the Spanish, who founded the earliest permanent colonial settlement at St. Augustine, in the territory they called Florida, in 1565. Spanish colonization—which lasted until 1821—produced a string of military outposts and missions from Florida to Virginia, into Louisiana, and from the Southwest territories into California.

In the North, enterprising Dutch fur traders arrived in the Hudson River Valley in 1610 and founded the colony of New Netherland in 1621. The term "Dutch Colonial" actually refers to an amalgam of building traditions brought to the region between the Connecticut and Delaware rivers by a broad range of immigrants, including the Dutch, Flemish, Swedes, French Huguenots, Walloons, and Prussians.

In the 1680s, a climate of religious tolerance began drawing German and Swiss settlers from the Lower Rhine palatinate to the Pennsylvania colony, as well as to areas of Virginia, Maryland, Delaware, and North Carolina. While many assimilated into the English culture already established (see Chapter Three), small separatist sects, including the Moravians, Amish, Dunkers, Schwenkfelders, and Mennonites, held on to a strong Germanic identity clearly evident in regional architecture.

French colonists first made their mark in 1682, when La Salle descended the Mississippi River. Consisting largely of trading posts dependent on Quebec, the upper region of the Mississippi Valley was known as the Illinois Country. In 1718 this became part of the Louisiana Territory, where the Acadians (French Canadians from Nova Scotia) and the Creoles (descendants of West Indian, French, and Spanish settlers) blended their own architectural vocabulary into a distinctive regional style.

The largest settlements in the Spanish Southeast grew around such military outposts as Pensacola and St. Augustine, Florida, which were built on a European grid plan. Walled houses fronted directly on the street; a door through the wall provided access to an enclosed yard, where one entered the house through a side or rear loggia, or roofed gallery. Along with hanging street balconies and galleries, these practical outdoor rooms usually faced southeast, to catch prevailing summer breezes and the warmth of the low winter sun. Many early homes in St. Augustine were built of coquina, an indigenous limestone made of shell aggregate the Spanish discovered on nearby Anastasia Island in 1583. Coated with tabby, a cement made of oyster shells and lime, coquina proved a durable and waterproof type of masonry.

In the Southwest the prevailing building material was the local clay adobe, mud mixed with a chopped straw binder and used as plaster or sun-dried in bricks. Here the Spanish concept of the enclosed household found expression in large, self-contained ranchos and haciendas. One of the most distinctive features of Spanish architecture in this region is the *fogón*, a bell-shaped corner fireplace.

PLANK HOUSE (CASA DE TABLAS) (FLORIDA TERRITORY)

crossed-pole thatch weight · smoke hole · cabbage palm thatch (*palma* or *guano*) · gable · vertical plank door

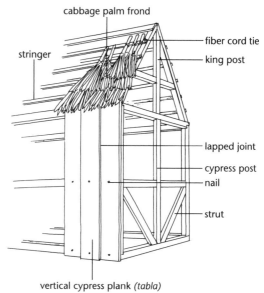

cabbage palm frond · stringer · fiber cord tie · king post · lapped joint · cypress post · nail · strut · vertical cypress plank (*tabla*)

Anatomy of Tabby Wall Construction

removable dowel

fourth pour

lime mortar with sand and oyster-shell aggregate (tabby)

board
pin

third pour

second pour

first pour

A tabby wall was raised by setting two boards on edge. Into this frame was then poured limeshell mortar mixed with sand and oyster shells. When that section had set, the boards were raised a level and the process repeated.

FLAT-ROOFED HOUSE (AZOTEA) (FLORIDA TERRITORY)

cypress shingles

clay rainspout (canale)

window grating (reja)

whitewashed plaster over tabby

vertical plank door

**STREET HOUSE
(FLORIDA TERRITORY)**

hipped roof

cypress shingles *(rajones)*

louvered
shutter

window
grating
(reja)

second-story
gallery

whitewashed plaster over quar-
ried shell aggregate (coquina)

vertical plank door

rear loggia

side
court-
yard

street entrance

Spanish Colonial

ZAGÚAN (SOUTHWEST)

beam *(viga)*

plaster over adobe brick

crossbeam

wide gate (for wagons)

batten

narrow door (for humans)

strap hinge

Surrounded by a windowless adobe wall, the large fortresslike hacienda of the Southwest housed not only numerous members of the extended Spanish family, but also farmhands and livestock. Arranged contiguously, household rooms opened onto a front courtyard, called a *placita*. A back courtyard served as a corral, where barns, storerooms, and animal sheds were located. A massive front gate opened into a covered passage, or *zagúan*, wide enough for a wagon to pass through.

HACIENDA PLAN

livestock

livestock

storage

poultry

corral

storage

courtyard *(placita)*

well

covered passage *(zagúan)*

gate

BELL-SHAPED FIREPLACE (FOGÓN)

peeled aspen or cottonwood pole *(latia)*

beam *(viga)*

loft bed

hood

chimney (plaster over adobe brick)

stone cooktop

oven

hearth

COOKING FIREPLACE (FOGÓN DE CAMPAGNA)

chimney

adobe

hearth

HEATING FIREPLACE (FOGÓN DE PADERCITA)

chimney

little wall *(padercita)*

adobe

hearth

Spanish Colonial

shell

adobe wall

butt hinge

rosette

shutting stile

hanging stile

chip carvings

bottom rail

Roman arch

top rail

top rail

spindle

butt hinge

slats

shutting stile

hanging stile

shutting stile

adobe wall

inset panel

hanging stile

strap hinge   bottom rail

bottom rail

URBAN HOUSE
(NEW AMSTERDAM)

storage loft

gable

clay barrel tiles

hoisting
bracket

corbie-step
(crow-stepped
gable)

brick relieving
arch
(segmented)

vertical
plank shutter

brick
masonry

diamond-
pane
casement

transom
light

paneled
double door

bulkhead

rubblework
masonry

Architecture in the Dutch colony was defined by distinctive regional character-istics that lingered in more isolated areas for at least a century after the British gained control in 1664. The principal house type of the two commercial centers, New Amsterdam (New York) and Fort Orange (Albany), was the narrow town house, which faced gable end to the street and often included a store-front and a storage loft. In these urban areas, law required a brick veneer over the timber frame for fire pro-tection. Stone houses were more prevalent in the lower Hudson Valley, while the clapboarded Flemish farm-house with flared roof eaves was local to southern New York, Long Island, and north-ern New Jersey.

A notable feature of early Dutch buildings was a hooded fireplace (with no jambs, or side walls), fitted with a cloth mantel skirt to keep smoke in. The Dutch also introduced the distinctive anchorbent framing and the wide aisle barn, with doors on the gable ends, to the New World.

Dutch Colonial

BRICK HOUSE (ALBANY)

chimney cap

flat-head (shed-roofed) dormer

shed roof

shingles

gambrel roof

gable

molded brick belt course

tumbling (mouse-tooth) brickwork

flat (gauged) arch

brick masonry

molded brick water table

rubblework foundation

twelve-over-twelve double-hung sash

divided door

JAMBLESS (SIDELESS) FIREPLACE

anchor beam

mantel

hood

corbel brace (*korbeel*)

whitewash over plaster

cloth skirt

tile facing

post

cast-iron fireback

hearthstone

FLEMISH FARMHOUSE
(NEW JERSEY & LONG ISLAND)

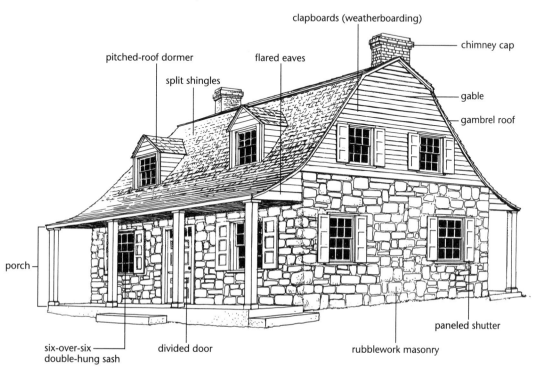

clapboards (weatherboarding)

chimney cap

pitched-roof dormer

flared eaves

split shingles

gable

gambrel roof

porch

paneled shutter

six-over-six
double-hung sash

divided door

rubblework masonry

porch

chamber

chamber

kitchen

parlor

porch

Dutch Colonial

**STONE HOUSE
(HUDSON VALLEY)**

split shingles

steep pitched roof

brick gable

flared eaves

paneled shutter

divided door

twelve-over-twelve double-hung sash

rubblework masonry

kitchen

parlor

DIVIDED DOOR

top rail
bull's-eye window
shutting stile
keyhole
shelf molding
fielded (raised) panels
bottom rail
strap hinge
bull's-eye window
hanging stile
lock plate
horizontal plank

(EXTERIOR)   (INTERIOR)

DIVIDED DOOR   **FULL DOOR**

transom light
strap hinge
diagonal plank
transom light
drop latch
vertical plank
light
cornice molding
latch (uses no key)
battens

top rail
knocker
shutting stile
shelf molding
fielded (raised) panel
bottom rail
lock plate

(EXTERIOR)   (INTERIOR)   (EXTERIOR)   (INTERIOR)

Anatomy of a Dutch Anchorbent Frame

peg

rafter

collar beam

tie beam

queen post

front plate

strut

corbel brace (*korbeel*)

H-shaped bent

anchor beam

sill

end post

ANCHOR-BEAM BENT DETAIL

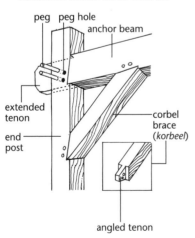

peg   peg hole

anchor beam

extended tenon

corbel brace (*korbeel*)

end post

angled tenon

One of the most distinctive features of Dutch Colonial architecture was the anchorbent frame. This extremely stable system for framing with structural timbers relied on H-shaped bents formed by two end posts connected with a horizontal anchor beam. These anchor-beam bents were arranged in multiples down the length of the building, connected by a sill at the bottom and a plate at the top. The beam tenon often extended beyond the end posts, and the corbel brace had an angled tenon so that it could be wedged firmly into the post for extra rigidity (see detail, *left*).

AISLE BARN

projecting bay

hayloft

split shingles

gable

pitched roof

clapboards
(weatherboarding)

vertical plank doors

storage
(wood floor)

harness room
(dirt floor)

entry
(dirt floor)

stall
(wood floor)

storage
(wood floor)

wagon storage
(wood floor)

trough

stall
(dirt floor)

German/Swiss Colonial

Germanic housing in the colonies was typically well built and designed for efficiency. One of the earliest Germanic building types in Pennsylvania was the tripartite house, which reflected the Old World tradition of combining a house, a threshing area, and a stable under the same roof. For convenience, a springhouse was often incorporated directly into a dwelling, which might also include an attic meat-smoking room, or *Rauchkammer,* connected to the chimney stack. Particularly practical building types were the bank house and bank barn, built into a ground slope to provide cool lower-level storage rooms.

The majority of early Germanic houses in America were simple, well-built log dwellings, although it is mostly the stone buildings that have survived. Stone, considered a status symbol, was favored primarily by the rural gentry. The typical Germanic plan was an asymmetrical three-room layout, placing the kitchen (*Kich,* in Pennsylvania German) on the main level, usually to the right of the chimney. To the left was the stove room (*Schtupp*), with a sleeping chamber (*Kammer*) in the rear. By the mid-1700s, many Germanic settlers had adopted the Georgian center-hall plan (page 76).

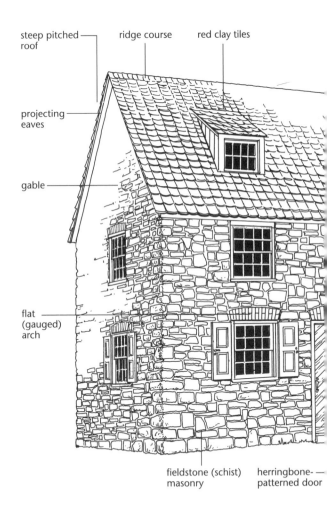

steep pitched roof — ridge course — red clay tiles

projecting eaves

gable

flat (gauged) arch

fieldstone (schist) masonry

herringbone-patterned door

chimney cap

flat-head (shed-roofed) dormer

vertical plank barn siding

barn vent

paneled shutter

divided door

double-hung sash

vertical plank door

German/Swiss Colonial

LOG HOUSE

red clay tiles

rubblework chimney

vertical plank siding

plank shutter

plaster chinking

hewn logs

rubblework foundation

V-notch

flared eaves

deep overhang (to shade porch)

extended joists

vertical plank door

batten

porch (*Vorhuf*)

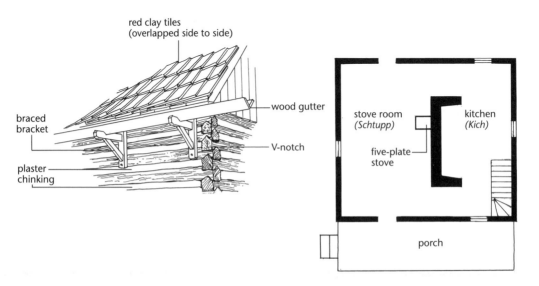

red clay tiles (overlapped side to side)

braced bracket

plaster chinking

wood gutter

V-notch

stove room (*Schtupp*)

kitchen (*Kich*)

five-plate stove

porch

SWISS BANK HOUSE

pitched roof

gable

red clay tiles

nine-over-six
double-hung sash

porch (*Vorhuf*)

brick relieving arch
(segmented)

fieldstone
(schist)
masonry

divided door

ground slope

exterior stone stair (*Freitreppe*)

sleeping chamber
(*Kammer*)

sleeping
room
(*Kammer*)

stove room
(*Schtupp*)

The Swiss bank house was typically
built with the gable end set into the
ground slope. The kitchen was located
on the lower level, with a rear room
dug into the earth. Many of the Swiss
settlers were distillers and stored their
brews in this cool space.

German/Swiss Colonial

GERMANIC FIREPLACE

mantel

bracket

inset kettle

soup hearth
(*Suppenherd*)

mantel

soup hearth
(*Suppenherd*)

raised brick hearth

SECTION VIEW

coal chute
(to stove)

five-plate
cast-iron stove

raised brick
hearth

cast relief

wall dividing
kitchen and
stove room

five-plate
cast-iron stove

stone block

The Germanic house in America featured an ingenious fireplace arrangement. Hot coals were shoveled through a hole in the back of the cooking fireplace directly into a five-plate cast-iron stove, which was used to warm the parlor or "stove room" (which backed up to the kitchen). An important symbol of domesticity, the iron stove was smokeless, permitting white walls, highly desirable for a parlor. The cooking fireplace usually had a raised soup hearth, or *Suppenherd*, which required less bending, and less wood to keep hot, than the open English hearth.

SPRINGHOUSE DWELLING

ridge course

pitched roof

red clay tiles

vertical plank siding

rubblework chimney

gable

flared eaves

six-over-six double-hung sash

extended joist

divided door

porch (*Vorhuf*)

rubblework

whitewashed plaster over stone masonry

door to springhouse

spring

sleeping room (*Kammer*)

kitchen (*Kich*)

five-plate stove

stove room (*Schtupp*)

Anatomy of a Germanic Roof Frame

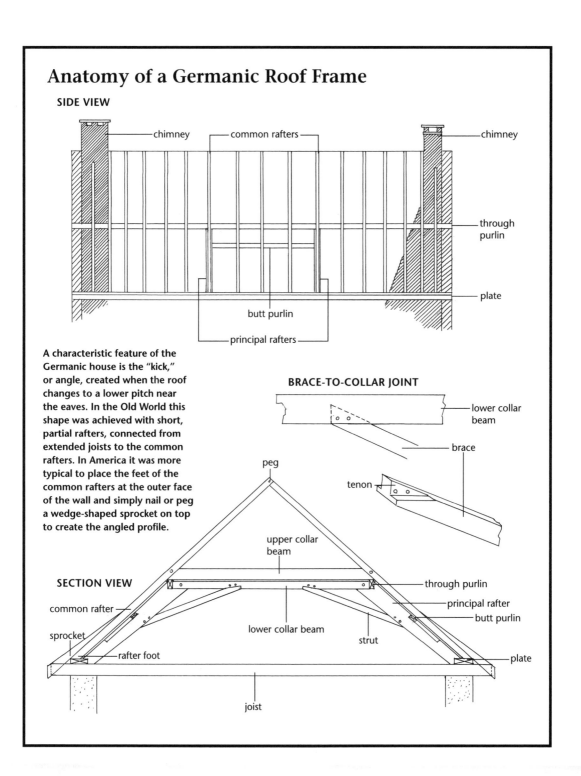

SIDE VIEW

chimney

common rafters

chimney

through purlin

plate

butt purlin

principal rafters

A characteristic feature of the Germanic house is the "kick," or angle, created when the roof changes to a lower pitch near the eaves. In the Old World this shape was achieved with short, partial rafters, connected from extended joists to the common rafters. In America it was more typical to place the feet of the common rafters at the outer face of the wall and simply nail or peg a wedge-shaped sprocket on top to create the angled profile.

BRACE-TO-COLLAR JOINT

lower collar beam

brace

tenon

peg

upper collar beam

SECTION VIEW

common rafter

sprocket

rafter foot

lower collar beam

strut

through purlin

principal rafter

butt purlin

plate

joist

German/Swiss Colonial

CENTER-HALL HOUSE

split shingles (shakes)

gable

pent roof

kick

boxed eaves

balcony

twelve-over-twelve double-hung sash

fieldstone (schist)

divided door

transom

paneled shutter

exterior stone stair (*Freitreppe*)

sleeping chamber (*Kammer*)

kitchen (*Kich*)

stove opening

parlor

hall

stove room (*Schtupp*)

German/Swiss Colonial

PAINTED WALL PATTERNS

Boldly painted wall patterns illustrate the Germanic preference for graphic interior decorations. Sponged dots, squibs, spirals, and cross-hatching were painted directly on plaster walls in black, white, and maroon, with woodwork in deep blue, salmon, and bright yellow. The patterns shown here were discovered painted on the wainscot of the 1758 Peter Wenz house in Worcester, Pennsylvania.

BAKE OVEN

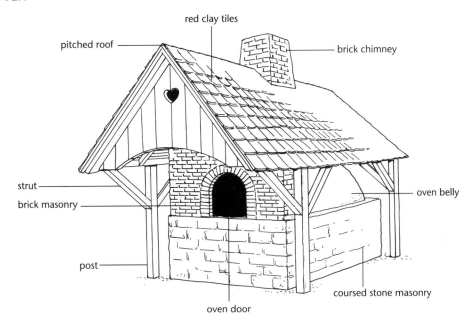

red clay tiles

pitched roof

brick chimney

strut

brick masonry

post

oven door

oven belly

coursed stone masonry

Few Germanic households were without a bake oven, often a separate outbuilding that might be incorporated into a larger smokehouse, washhouse, or summer kitchen. The outdoor oven was considered safer than its indoor counterpart, and its larger hearth permitted greater baking yields—as many as a dozen loaves of bread and even more pies at a time. The overhanging roof often shaded cooling shelves.

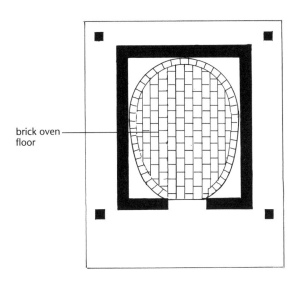

brick oven floor

German/Swiss Colonial

BANK BARN (FRONT VIEW)

vertical plank barn siding

vent

rubblework masonry

ground slope

window grille

UPPER LEVEL

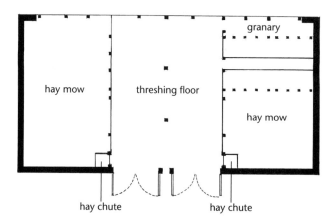

granary

hay mow

threshing floor

hay mow

hay chute

hay chute

BANK BARN (REAR VIEW)

vent

eaves

vent

segmented arch

ground slope

split shingles

vertical plank barn siding

hanging slider

rubblework masonry

divided door

forebay overhang

LOWER LEVEL

wine cellar

cattle pen

horse stall

French Colonial

brick chimney

double-pitched
(broken-pitched)
hipped roof

porch
(galerie)

plank porch
flooring

log post

casement window
(glass, linen, or paper lights)

stones and lime mortar (pierrotage)
or mud and grass plaster (bousillage)

The early houses of both the Illinois Country and the Louisiana Territory shared two distinct characteristics: the steep hipped Norman pavilion roof and the four-sided porch (*galerie*), which gave the roof a second (broken) pitch partway down. One basic house type, the *maison de poteaux-en-terre*, was built on upright posts driven into the ground; the other, the *maison de poteaux-sur-solle*, had a massive timber frame built directly on a sill. Both types used a fill of either stones and lime mortar (*pierrotage*) or a mud plaster bound with grass or Spanish moss (*bousillage*). The exterior was usually plastered.

The early French plan was a two-room, center-chimney layout. As houses grew larger, this evolved into a single or double row of rooms placed end to end with interior chimneys located at the gable ends. Rooms opened directly out onto the porch—there were seldom interior halls—by means of full-length casements. In the bayou areas of Louisiana, the house was typically raised as much as two feet to keep out moisture; riverside plantation houses were raised about seven feet. The kitchen was in a separate building.

decorative finial
(*épi*)

plank shutter

split cypress shingles

rafter tails

french door (full-length casement)

whitewashed plaster

fill of stones and lime mortar
(*pierrotage*) or mud and
grass plaster (*bousillage*)

post (red cedar,
cypress, or
mulberry)

post hewn flat
above ground line

whole post below
ground line

vertical post set in
one-foot-deep
trench

**POSTS-IN-GROUND
(POTEAUX-EN-TERRE)
INTERIOR VIEW**

Possibly derived from the Caribbean or the Gulf of
Mexico, the *poteaux-en-terre* building method was
the most common in the French territories. This
technique did not involve true framing; instead,
logs (mulberry or rot-resistant cedar or cypress)
were placed upright at three- or four-inch intervals
in a one-foot-deep trench. The trench was then
backfilled, and the uprights, which were hewn flat
above the ground, were secured at the tops with a
plate for additional stability.

French Colonial

**RAISED PLANTATION HOUSE
(LOUISIANA TERRITORY)**

chimney cap

brick chimney

split cypress shingles

porch (galerie)

French door
(full-length casement)

FRENCH DOORS

molding

light   muntin

batten

inset panel

vertical plank shutter

decorative finial
(*épi*)

pitched-roof dormer

double-pitched
(broken-pitched)
hipped roof

transom

clapboards
(weatherboarding)

pier

whitewashed plaster over
mud between posts
(*bousillage-entre-poteaux*)

| bedroom | bedroom | parlor | bedroom | bedroom |
| bedroom | | | | bedroom |

porch (*galerie*)

Anatomy of a Norman Truss

strut

purlins

king post

rafter

collar beam

The technique for framing the steeply pitched "Norman" roof characteristic of French colonial architecture was brought to the Illinois Country from Quebec Province by Canadian carpenters. The steep pitch was intended to shed water from thatch, but was retained even after shingles became the common roof covering. The vertical king post was usually crowned by a decorative finial (*épi*). Several houses with this type of roof framing, typically of oak, still exist in Ste. Genevieve, Missouri.

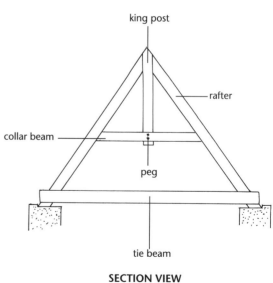

king post

rafter

collar beam

peg

tie beam

SECTION VIEW

MAISON DE POTEAUX-SUR-SOLLE

split cypress shingles

hipped roof

framing timber (red cedar, cypress, or mulberry)

strap hinge   casement   sill *(solle)*   cypress pier

plank shutter

mud between posts
(bousillage-entre-poteaux)

DOOR HARDWARE

INTERIOR LATCHES

RAM'S HORN HINGE

Among the distinctive hardware used in the French Colonial period was the ram's horn hinge *(left)*. Long interior latches *(above)* were necessary to secure the tops of French and double paneled doors. A shorter version of the same latch was used for the door bottoms.

French Colonial

**RAISED HOUSE
(LOUISIANA TERRITORY)**

split cypress shingles

hipped roof

cypress logs

stone pier

six-over-six double-hung sash

clapboards

paneled shutter

French door (full-length casement)

vertical plank door

porch (*galerie*)

colonnette

dining room

bedroom

parlor

bedroom

porch (*galerie*)

LOG HOUSE
(ILLINOIS COUNTRY)

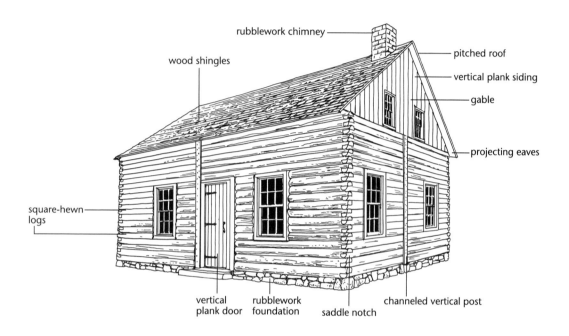

rubblework chimney

pitched roof

vertical plank siding

gable

wood shingles

projecting eaves

square-hewn logs

vertical plank door

rubblework foundation

saddle notch

channeled vertical post

CHANNELED POST DETAIL

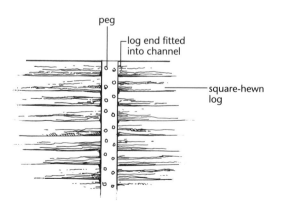

peg

log end fitted into channel

square-hewn log

French Colonial log construction featured an unusual system in which one end of a log was notched at the building corners and the other end was set in a vertical post placed at or near the center of each wall. A three-inch-deep channel ran along both sides of the post; each end of a log was hewed to fit the channel and pegged into place. This made it possible to build longer walls out of the shorter logs typically available in the northern Mississippi Valley.

French Colonial

BARN

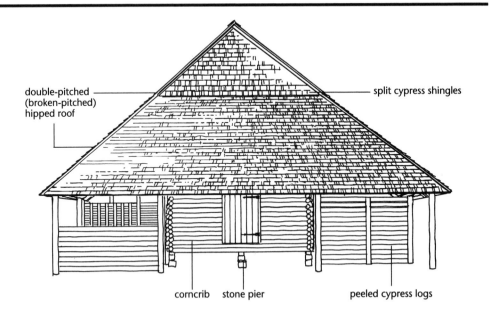

double-pitched (broken-pitched) hipped roof

split cypress shingles

corncrib   stone pier

peeled cypress logs

storage   storage

(dirt floor)

corncrib (cypress plank floor)

porch (galerie)

PIGEONNIER

decorative finial (*épi*)

split cypress shingles

hipped roof

ridge course

end (corner) post

cypress clapboards (*bousillage*)

paneled door

stone pier

The *pigeonnier,* or pigeon cote, was a common feature of the French Colonial plantation house, which often boasted two of these roosting houses, placed symmetrically in front and back of the main residence. A typical *pigeonnier* was one-and-a-half or two stories high, with the setting (nesting) boxes placed over a ground-floor storeroom; fancy versions featured octagonal designs. The birds were raised for both meat and fertilizer.

SECTION VIEW

decorative finial (*épi*)

crossbeam
cypress post

setting boxes

joist

cross brace

corner post

sill (*solle*)
stone pier

Chapter Three
Early English Colonial

Establishing their first settlements in Jamestown, Virginia, in 1607, and Plymouth, Massachusetts, in 1620, some half a million colonists had emigrated to America from England, Scotland, and Ireland by the end of the 17th century. With them came a thoroughly British pattern of social and cultural values that soon traversed the Atlantic seaboard.

Building characteristics varied from colony to colony and town to town. However, a broad distinction can be drawn between the New England village, which comprised individual houses grouped around a town green, and the isolated southern plantation, a self-sufficient enterprise supported by slave labor and complete with a forge, carpentry shop, and perhaps a brickyard. New England settlers were primarily middle-class yeoman families. Most came from a single area of England (East Anglia), and they continued a well-entrenched tradition of heavytimber-framed buildings. Settlers of the Virginia tidewater region and farther south came from more diverse areas and included a significant number of bricklayers and masons. Lime, used for mortar, was also readily available in the South, so masonry construction was more typical.

Until about 1700, all early English Colonial houses shared a distinct postmedieval character, most noticeable in steep pitched roofs (a holdover originally designed to support thatch), immense stacked chimneys, and small casement windows. The plan was typically a one-room, all-purpose "fireroom," or "hall," used for cooking, eating, and sleeping, or a two-room layout with a central chimney dividing the hall and parlor or kitchen. Additional sleeping chambers were located above.

VILLAGE HOUSE (NEW ENGLAND)

split shingles (shakes)
of pine, hemlock, cedar, or oak

chimney cap

rubblework chimney

valley

intersecting gable

steep pitched roof

gable

overhang (jetty)

diamond-pane casement

end (corner) post

riven clapboards
(weatherboarding)
of cedar, oak, or white pine

porch

pendant
(pendill or drop)

divided door

rubblework foundation

porch

parlor

hall

porch

A mark of late Elizabethan architecture, the overhang, or jetty, was a feature of early Colonial houses throughout the 1600s, primarily in towns and cities. In England it may have been used to provide shelter over street-level market stalls, but in America the shallower overhang—four to six inches deep—was apparently a purely decorative holdover.

Early English Colonial

SALTBOX
(NEW ENGLAND)

chimney cap

rubblework chimney

gable

split shingles
(shakes)

saltbox roof

rear lean-to

end (corner) post

overhang (jetty)

pendant
(pendill or drop)

vertical plank door

diamond-pane casement

riven clapboards
(weatherboarding)

kitchen (rear) lean-to

parlor

hall

porch

CLAPBOARD DETAIL

clapboard

bead

end post

PENDANTS

Common during the second half of the 17th century, wood pendants (also called pendills or drops) were used to finish the lower ends of the front second-story posts that framed an overhang. Purely decorative, pendants offered a place for the woodcarver to try out different designs. The overhang and pendants seldom, if ever, appeared on the rear of a structure. These oak examples survive from late 17th-century houses in Connecticut and Massachusetts.

tenon

tenon

pinhole

tenon

Early English Colonial

chimney cap

stacked chimney

ridge

valley

intersecting gable

split shingles (shakes)

saltbox roof

projecting eaves

fixed diamond-pane sash

vertical plank door

pegged window frame

rubblework masonry

riven clapboards (weatherboarding)

end (corner) post

kitchen

hall

Anatomy of a Post-and-Beam Frame

principal rafters (over post)

common rafters

drawbore pin

attic joist

mortise for joist

front plate

end girt

front girt

end (corner) post

sill

chimney girt

cellar girt

post

joists

butt purlin

collar beam

rear plate

end girt

rear girt

end girt

summer beam

sill

end (corner) post

Timber framing was based on a fundamental system in which uprights (posts) were supported by horizontal members (beams) and filled with brick and clay. All framing members were joined by means of a mortise (socket or groove) and tenon (tongue) joint secured with wooden drawbore pins; no glue was ever used. The holes in the mortise and tenon were slightly misaligned so that when the pin was driven in, it forced the holes into line, creating a firm joint.

SECTION VIEW

wooden drawbore pin

pinhole

shoulder

cheek

tenon

shoulder

tenon

pin-hole

pin-hole

cheek

mortise

Early English Colonial

PLANTATION HOUSE (SOUTHERN TIDEWATER)

ridge course (of shingles)

split shingles (shakes)

chimney cap

steep pitched roof

pitched-roof dormer

gable

riven clapboards (weatherboarding)

dormer

projecting eaves

flat (gauged) arch

rowlock course (row of bricks laid end out)

diamond-pane casement

divided door

brick relieving arch (segmented)

molded brick water table

hall

parlor

ENGLISH BOND

FLEMISH BOND

COMMON BOND

DUTCH CROSS BOND

To make a strong wall, bricks are laid in a three-dimensional bonding system that also creates a decorative face. In the early Colonial period, two types of bonds typically used in England were often adopted in the New World. The English bond alternated rows, or courses, of bricks set as headers (ends showing) and stretchers (sides showing). The Flemish bond alternated headers and stretchers in the same course. Other typical bonds included the common bond and Dutch cross bond.

Early English Colonial

PLANTATION HOUSES
(MID-ATLANTIC AND SOUTH)

intersecting gable —

inset double arches

turned spin‹

linked chimney caps

rowlock course
(row of bricks laid end out)

diagonally set chimney stack

chimney viewer

steeply-pitched hipped roof

corbeled cornice

split shingles (shakes)

flat (gauged) arch

diamond-
pane
casement

molded brick water table

brick relieving arch
(segmented)

ridge course

overhang (jetty)

pitched-roof dormer

gable

valley

split wood shingles (shakes)

riven clapboards (weatherboarding)

porch

pegged window frame

six-over-six double-hung sash

porch

kitchen

hall

parlor

bench — porch

Early English Colonial

HALL (FIREROOM)

summer beam

chamfer

chimney girt

joists

chamfer stop (lamb's tongue)

fireplace lintel

plate

fixed diamond-pane sash

crease-molded paneling

hearthstone

rubblework masonry

ENTRY STAIR

raised (fielded) panel

banister

newel cap

newel post

turned baluster

riser

string

tread

(Opposite page) **Leaded-glass windows persisted well into the second quarter of the 1700s and were typically either fixed or hinged casements (double-hung sashes were rare). English casements were set on the outside of the window opening and opened outward; they were never used with shutters. During the 1600s most glass used in the colonies was imported from England. Bubbled glass was considered inferior; clear, high-quality "crown" glass could cost fifteen times as much and was thus reserved for rooms in the front of the finest houses.**

DOORS (INTERIOR)

scratch-and-punch decoration

top rail

hanging stile

peg

molding

inset panel

hinge pin

hinge leaf

bottom rail

strap hinge

crease molding

top rail

latch

inset panel

strap hinge

bottom rail

WINDOWS (EXTERIOR)

casement

stay bar

diamond pane (quarrel)

stile

lead came (divider)

casement

stay bar

fixed window

peg

mullions

lead came (divider)

diamond pane (quarrel)

rail

stile

peg

fixed window sash

lead came (divider)

stile

ventilating grille with sliding shutter

Anatomy of a Purlin Roof Frame

The pitched roof of a timber-framed house was constructed with slanting rafters, covered with horizontal roof boards and a final sheathing of shingles. The sturdiest framing method was the purlin system, in which principal rafters, placed over posts in the lower frame, were joined by horizontal purlins and mortised into a ridge pole.

BARN

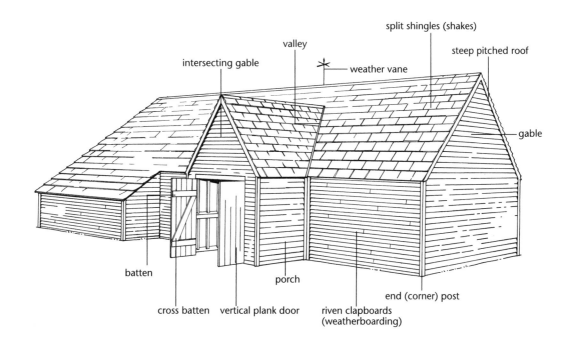

split shingles (shakes)

steep pitched roof

valley

intersecting gable

weather vane

gable

batten

porch

cross batten   vertical plank door

end (corner) post

riven clapboards
(weatherboarding)

milking
passage

storage

threshing
floor

cow house

manuring
passage

porch

Chapter Four
The Georgian Era

The term "Georgian" generally refers to a period of architectural development in America from about 1700 to the Revolution (during the reigns of kings George I, II, and III). Rooted in the Classical design principles of ancient Rome, this English style came to America by way of British pattern books and an ever-swelling wave of masons, carpenters, and joiners who emigrated from England.

With its rigid symmetry, balanced proportion, and Classical detailing, the Georgian mode represented a final break from medieval architecture. Formal and dignified, it transcended geographical boundaries and was enthusiastically adopted for the imposing seaport mansions of New England's wealthy mercantile class, southern manors and plantation houses, and vernacular backcountry farmhouses, whose door and window designs were often copied directly from the pages of a carpenter's handbook. Surface ornament, usually concentrated on the centrally placed entry, was especially lavish during the early, Baroque phase of the style. A more academic, restrained approach in the mid- to late 1700s adhered more closely to the strict design principles of the Italian architect Andrea Palladio (1508–80).

As the notions of privacy and leisure time developed during the 1700s, the symmetrical Georgian center-hall plan evolved with larger rooms as well as more rooms designed for specialized uses, such as the dining room and library. The increasing availability of white lime plaster resulted in more sculptural interior ornament, often producing elaborate precast cornices and ceiling medallions.

**MANOR HOUSE
(MID-ATLANTIC)**

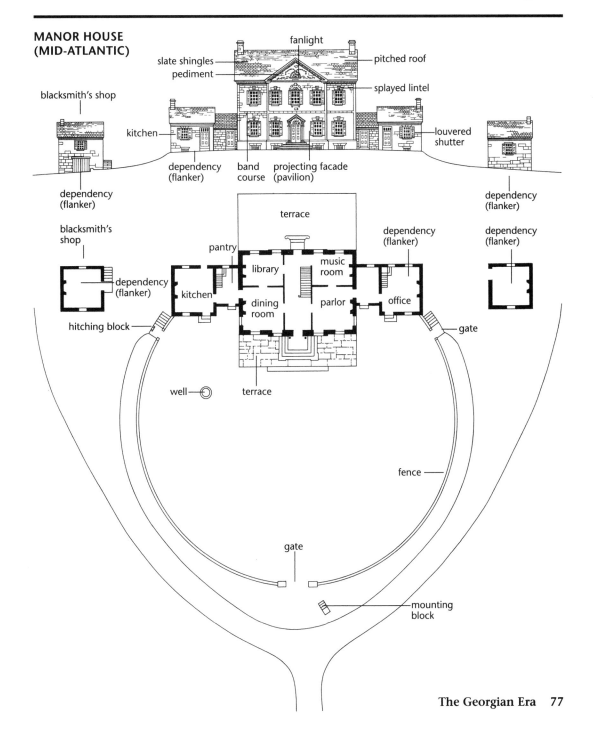

blacksmith's shop

slate shingles
pediment

fanlight

pitched roof

splayed lintel

kitchen

louvered shutter

dependency (flanker)

dependency (flanker)

dependency (flanker)

band course

projecting facade (pavilion)

blacksmith's shop

dependency (flanker)

dependency (flanker)

dependency (flanker)

terrace

pantry

dependency (flanker)

library

music room

kitchen

dining room

parlor

office

hitching block

gate

well

terrace

fence

gate

mounting block

Georgian

**PLANTATION HOUSE
(MID-ATLANTIC AND SOUTH)**

roundel

hip molding

pediment

raking cornice

projecting facade (pavilion)

clapboards
(weatherboarding)

hipped roof

dependency (flanker)

hyphen

water table

lattice

portico (Doric order)

portico

library

salon

with-
drawing
room

dependency (flanker)

dining
room

salon

parlor

hyphen

hyphen

kitchen

portico

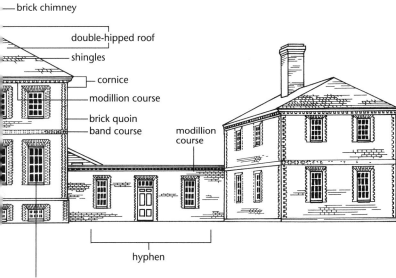

brick chimney

double-hipped roof

shingles

cornice

modillion course

brick quoin
band course

modillion
course

hyphen

six-over-six double-hung sash

DOUBLE-HUNG SASH DETAIL

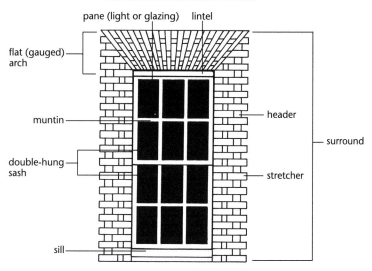

pane (light or glazing)   lintel

flat (gauged)
arch

muntin

double-hung
sash

sill

header

surround

stretcher

Pattern Book Designs

Pediments of continued Cornices.

B. Langley Invent 1740. *T.L. Sculp.*

Ogee Scheme Pediment.

Triple Curved Pediment.

B. Langley Invent 1740. *T.L. Sculp.*

The most widely used 18th-century architectural books in both England and America were by the prolific English author Batty Langley (1696–1751), who wrote more than twenty practical handbooks designed for the average carpenter. These plates are from *The Builder's Jewel*, published in eleven editions from 1741 to 1787.

Ionick Modilion at large.

Ionick Dentules at large.

B.L. Invent 1741. *T. Langley Sculp.*

Georgian

END HOUSE (CHARLESTON)

pedimented dormer

brick (common bond)

stone quoin

splayed lintel

flat (gauged) arch

cornice

keystone

stone band course

keystone

fanlight

Gibbs surround (protruding stone door enframement with keystone)

two-story Doric portico

coping

rowlock course (bricks laid end out)

six-over-six double-hung sash

water table

Georgian

**MANOR HOUSE
(NEW ENGLAND)**

returning cornice — chimney cap

brick chimney

pediment

shingles

pedimented dormer

gambrel roof

gable

twelve-over-twelve
double-hung sash

tympanum

flared eaves

Palladian window

projecting facade
(pavilion)

dentiled lintel

eared (crossetted)
surround

Ionic
portico

porch

six-over-six sidelight

wooden quoin

clapboards (weatherboarding)

porch

kitchen

dining
room

library

parlor

parlor

Anatomy of a Gambrel Roof Frame

The gambrel roof was introduced to the English colonies as early as the 1640s and was widely used in Georgian-period building, particularly in the North. The two-pitched roof is defined by a short upper slope and a second, long slope down to the plate. The gambrel offered more headroom than a pitched roof of the same height, but it was more complex structurally, so it cost more.

SEAPORT HOUSE (NEW ENGLAND)

Georgian

FARMHOUSE (NEW ENGLAND)

- pitched roof
- gable
- cornice
- plaster over stone chimney
- split wood shingles (shakes)
- modillion course
- pediment
- splayed lintel
- plaster over stone masonry foundation
- clapboards (weatherboarding)
- fanlight
- twelve-over-twelve double-hung window

FARMHOUSE (MID-ATLANTIC)

- pitched roof
- raking cornice
- gable
- cornice
- keystone
- modillion course
- lead stars
- pediment
- fanlight
- Doric pilaster
- masonry foundation
- ashlar (squared building stone)

kitchen

parlor

FIREPLACE WALLS

dentil course · overmantel · modillion course

cornice · pediment · tympanum · ear (crossette) · Ionic pilaster · raised (fielded) panel · mantel · metopes · Doric pilaster · triglyphs · firebox

cornice · dentil course · broken pediment · ear (crossette) · raised (fielded) panel · pilaster · mantel · marble facing · firebox

Doric pilaster · tombstone panel · raised (fielded) panels · cornice

fanlight · built-in cupboard · paneled door (concealed)

mantel · firebox

Anatomy of a Double-Hung Sash (Interior)

The earliest known American example of the sliding, or double-hung, sash, which worked with pulleys, cords, and counterweights, occurred in Boston in 1703. Probably Dutch in origin, the system was fine-tuned by the English. Sash and blind factories were common in American cities by the mid-1700s and the double-hung sash all but replaced the medieval casement in Georgian houses.

WINDOWS (EXTERIOR)

cornice

dentil course

pulvinated frieze

muntins

upper sash

lower sash

pane (light or glazing)

sill

keystone

fret (meander or Greek key)

ridge piece

shingles

pediment

Doric pilaster

muntin

upper sash

pane (light or glazing)

lower sash

sill

carved acorn decoration

scroll pediment

upper sash

lower sash

pane (light or glazing)

sill

tympanum

pediment

pane (light or glazing)

upper sash

lower sash

sill

Georgian

DOORS (EXTERIOR)

raking cornice — tympanum

pediment

entablature —

keystone —

Corinthian capital

fanlight

entablature —

Corinthian column

raised (fielded) panel

raised (fielded) panel

Doric pilaster

base block

threshold —

rosette — finial

swan's neck pediment

raking cornice — tympanum

pediment

Doric pilaster —

Doric column

top rail

raised (fielded) panel

inset panel

base block —

base block

bottom rails

threshold

threshold

GATES

globe finial

finial

baluster

paneled
hanging post

base block

acorn finial

pickets

rails

hanging post

hanging post

urn

rosette

swan's neck pediment

Doric pilaster

fretwork medallion

picket

Chapter Five
Neoclassical Styles

The Neoclassical movement developed in Europe, especially in England and France, in the mid-18th century and began making its impact on American design after the Revolution. Like the Georgian mode, the Neoclassical was rooted in Classical orders (page 98) and concepts of proportion and decoration, but it differed in that it was based on a new perception of ancient Rome and Greece as separate and very distinct civilizations, each with its own merits. Whereas architects of the English Renaissance—the basis of the Georgian style—regarded ancient Rome as the leading authority on design matters, a new respect for ancient Greece now challenged this viewpoint.

Interest in the design principles of the two different cultures coincided with the emergence of archaeology as a serious science—major excavations began at Herculaneum in 1783 and at Pompeii in 1793. There was also a new class of superbly illustrated books that recorded individual monuments, including the buildings of the Acropolis, in unprecedented detail. Especially influential was the four-volume *Antiquities of Athens*, by James Stuart and Nicholas Revett, published in London between 1762 and 1816. As archeological studies progressed, a clearer understanding emerged of both the Roman interest in surface ornament and systems of proportion and the Greek passion for geometry and practical spatial function.

In America, Neoclassicism evolved into two distinct styles. The post-Colonial Federal style, based on Roman prototypes, lasted roughly from the 1780s to the 1820s, and the Greek Revival, based on Greek prototypes, extended from about 1820 through the 1840s.

URBAN HOUSE
(MID-ATLANTIC)

hipped roof

three-over-six double-hung sash

split wood shingles

wood gutter

drainpipe

belt courses

six-over-six double-hung sash

pediment

entry lodge

cornice

brick masonry (Flemish bond)

flat (gauged) arch

brick relieving (segmented) arch

louvered shutter

lamp

fanlight

paneled door

wrought-iron fence

ashlar (squared building stone)

Thoroughly British, Federal architecture began as the signature style of America's wealthy mercantile class, primarily members of the Federalist aristocracy whose international business trade kept them closely linked to England despite independence. Chaste, conservative, and gracefully elegant, the style first appeared primarily in important coastal cities, but eventually was adapted everywhere in simpler, vernacular forms.

Brick was the material of choice for simplified Federal-style facades, marked by refined decorations and elongated proportions. The interiors showed a new interest in how rooms related to one another in terms of volume and shape; round and oval spaces appeared for the first time, and ellipses and curves were constantly set off against rectilinear surfaces. A symmetrical facade often belied a varied plan, with rooms placed according to need rather than the dictates of a formal design. Based on the English Adamesque style, interior decoration featured elegant carved swags and garlands and other Classical details.

Federal

hipped roof

half-round window

brick relieving (segmented) arch

modillion course

cornice

six-over-six double-hung sash

splayed lintel

Palladian window

fanlight

keystone

urn

paneled post

pickets

paneled door

sidelight

Corinthian portico

privy

servants' room

upper kitchen

drawing room

dining room

drawing room

CARRIAGE HOUSE

hipped roof

clock

six-over-six double-hung sash

paneled door

FIREPLACE WALL

cornice

frieze

modillion course

dentil course

carved wood entablature

modified triglyphs

rosettes

nine-over-nine double-hung sash

mantel

fan

ellipses

entablature

raised (fielded) panel

cupboard

Doric pilaster

firebox

stone facing

wainscot

FREESTANDING STAIR

banister

riser

scrolled face-string panel

baluster

face string

lip

STAIR PLAN

Federal

**ROW HOUSE
(NEW ENGLAND)**

CORNICE DETAIL

acanthus

cymatium

corona

bed molding

guttae

balustrade

cornice

casement window

wrought-iron balcony

Corinthian pilaster

six-over-six
double-hung sash

splayed lintel

patera

fanlight

flat lintel

portico
(Doric order)

Doric column

wrought-iron
fence

sidelight

paneled door

ashlar (squared building stone)

semicircular bay

Federal

URBAN HOUSE (CHARLESTON)

half-round window

projecting facade (pavilion)

hipped roof

keystone

tympanum

pediment

flat (gauged) arch

louvered shutter

six-over-six double-hung sash

fascia board

cornice

brick relieving (segmented) arch

garland

fanlight

splayed lintel

sidelight

belt course

recessed entry

pier

double stairs

PLANTATION HOUSE (SOUTH)

split wood shingles

pitched-roof dormer

pediment

fan

Gothic sash

tympanum

Ionic column

two-story (double) portico

Doric column

clapboards

nine-over-nine double-hung sash

fanlight

Federal

hipped roof

Chinese
Chippendale railing

widow's
walk

modillion
course

dentil course

cornice

Ionic pilaster

brick masonry
side wall

clapboards

six-over-six
double-hung
sash

semicircular portico
(Ionic order)

paneled door

PORTICO DETAIL

cornice

modillion bracket

soffit

dentil course

guilloche

abacus

capital

frieze

entablature

architrave

Ionic column

volute

soffit

**FARM HOUSE
(MID-ATLANTIC)**

gambrel roof

split wood shingles

fanlight

elliptical window

flared eaves

clapboards

porch

six-over-six
double-hung
sash

fanlight

lattice

brick ashlar

paneled shutter

FANLIGHT DETAIL

PORCH DETAIL

keystone

beaded swag

lead dividers

capital

fret
(meander
or Greek
key)

railing

squared
Doric
column

baluster

cornice

ellipse

swag

urn

rosette

base

The Basic Orders

DORIC

entabla-ture
cornice
frieze
architrave

capital

neck

cymatium
corona
triglyph

metope

guttae

echinus

shaft

base
plinth

(ROMAN)

metope
triglyph
guttae
abacus
echinus

(GREEK)

IONIC

dentil

abacus

volute

base
plinth

CORINTHIAN

modillion

acanthus

base
plinth

ENGAGED COLUMN

flute

PILASTER

flute

The arrangement of freestanding columns supporting a horizontal beam element, or entablature, is known as an order. Derived from Classical architecture, the three basic orders are the Doric, the Ionic, and the Corinthian. The Greek and Roman orders differed—most noticeably in the Doric (the Greek Doric has no base). While each order was meant to follow strict rules of scale and proportion, these were sometimes modified in vernacular interpretations.

DOORS (EXTERIOR)

lead divider

fanlight

guilloche molding

sidelight

raised (fielded) panel

colonettes

double doors

ellipse

rosette

entablature

mullion

transom light

pilaster

inset panels

gougework

spiral molding

double doors

stylized Doric frieze

stylized triglyph

rosette

sidelight

paneled pilasters

louvered shutter

Greek Revival

Whereas the Federal style derived from the Palladian ideal of ancient Roman design, the Greek Revival adhered strictly to the Greek orders and systems of proportions and ornament. Modeled on English precedents, the Greek Revival was imported from abroad to America and spread rapidly along the coast and into the frontier. Linked by an educated elite to the ideals of ancient Greek democracy, it became associated with the young American democratic government and was considered a natural choice for civic monuments.

As a stylistic influence, the Greek Revival filtered down to even the most modest of rural farmhouses. Grander houses generally featured a columned portico supporting a triangular pediment—as on a Greek temple. Country builders accomplished the same effect simply by turning the gable end of a house to the street, boxing in the gable with a triangular raking cornice, adding pilasters to the corners, and painting the building a pristine white.

URBAN HOUSE

ESTATE HOUSE (NEW ENGLAND)

frieze

egg-and-dart molding

fret (meander or Greek key)

tympanum

pitched roof

raking cornice

pediment

cornice

entablature

pediment

Ionic column

Doric pilaster

six-over-six double-hung sash

portico

STAIRWAY

anthemion (palmette)

arch

paneled soffit

face string

pilaster

lip

baseboard

riser

tread

EGG-AND-DART DETAIL

ANTHEMION DETAIL

Greek Revival

PLANTATION HOUSE (SOUTH)

- eared surround
- raking cornice
- tympanum
- pediment
- cymatium
- architrave
- frieze
- entablature
- dentil course
- soffit
- plate glass
- cast-iron canopy
- Corinthian pilaster
- French door (full-length casement)
- Corinthian portico
- round-arched transom
- louvered shutter

kitchen

service wing

- porch
- pocket door
- dining room
- music room
- porch
- parlor
- portico

FIREPLACE

- fret (meander or Greek key)
- mantel
- entablature
- Doric column (engaged)

PLANTATION HOUSE (SOUTH)

hipped roof

dentil course

modillion course

cornice

soffit

wood balcony

Doric portico

sidelight — transom light — louvered shutter — Doric pilaster

FIREPLACE

patera

mantel

ear (crossette)

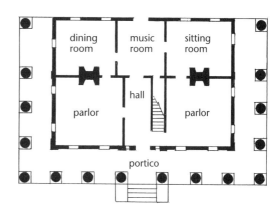

dining room

music room

sitting room

hall

parlor

parlor

portico

Greek Revival

**ROW HOUSE
(NEW ORLEANS)**

SECOND FLOOR

courtyard

service

bedroom

bedroom

parlor

FIRST FLOOR

courtyard

kitchen

porte cochère

shop

eyebrow window

parapet

cast-iron vent

soffit

cornice

drainpipe

lintel

cast-iron balcony

nine-over-nine double-hung sash

cast-iron bracket

entablature

cast-iron fence

Doric pilaster

DOORS (EXTERIOR)

anthemion (palmette)

entablature

volute

Ionic column

paneled door

leaded sidelight

leaded transom

anthemion (palmette)

entablature

Doric column

paneled door

egg-and-dart molding

ear (crossette)

acroterion

anthemia (palmettes)

sidelight

Doric column (engaged)

paneled door

fret (meander or Greek key)

transom light

sidelight

paneled door

Greek Revival

FARMHOUSE (MIDWEST)

- tympanum
- architrave
- raking cornice
- frieze
- pediment
- fascia
- pitched roof
- eyebrow window
- pediment
- six-over-six sash
- Doric portico
- rubblework foundation
- nine-over-six sash
- recessed porch
- paneled shutter
- clapboards

SEAPORT HOUSE (NEW ENGLAND)

- half-round window
- raking cornice
- six-over-six double-hung sash
- dentil course
- tympanum
- pitched roof
- cornice
- frieze
- architrave
- entablature
- clapboards
- entablature
- Doric pilasters

FARMHOUSE PLAN

- library
- pantry
- kitchen
- bed-room
- parlor
- parlor
- portico
- recessed porch

VILLA
(NEW ENGLAND)

hipped roof (ribbed tin) louvered shutter

frieze

painted garland

ashlar (squared building stone)

entab-lature

Doric pilaster

grisaille (trompe l'oeil) painting

rubblework foundation   cast-iron post   cast-iron balcony   veranda

French door (full-length casement)

The last phase of the Neoclassical mode in England—the Regency—was interpreted in American versions like this 1838 Connecticut house, which was possibly designed by an English architect. The painted swags and grisaille decorations of Classical urns and figures are thought to be the work of an itinerant French or Italian artist. The squared proportions of the house portend the villas that became so popular in the 1840s and 1850s (see pages 136–38).

servants' parlor

hall

servants' dining room

servants' kitchen

flower room

kitchen

conser-vatory

dining room

pantry

library

morning room

stair hall

entry

parlor   parlor

veranda

Chapter Six
Folk and Frontier Houses

Although architectural fashion has always been subject to the vagaries of contemporary taste, many regional building types in America were so well adapted to their specific locations that they endured even when the styles that formed them did not. Practical needs and available materials defined these so-called folk houses, whose distinctive forms—from the connected farms of northern Maine to the freestanding Conch houses of southern Florida—often reflected several different styles over the generations.

Most folk types outside of Colonial New England were the direct result of the great era of territorial expansion in the 19th century. With public land selling at $2.00 an acre, nearly one million settlers had spread into the vast area between the Appalachian Mountains and the Mississippi River by 1800. Texas was annexed in 1845, Florida gained statehood in the same year, and at the close of the Mexican War in 1848 the United States had possession of the territories of New Mexico and California.

Changing technology played a major role in shaping many new building types during this period. By the 1850s, cheap mass-produced nails became widely available, as did the circular saw, which was capable of milling vast quantities of lumber. Coinciding with the invention of the lightweight balloon frame (see page 127), these developments resulted in an unprecedented building boom of inexpensive frame houses across the country during the next decade.

Some vernacular traditions, such as the *Fachwerk* construction of German immigrants, reflected a specific ethnic heritage; others, such as sod and adobe houses, demonstrated the use of local building material. While often very different from one another, all types of folk houses shared one characteristic: common sense.

Cape Cod Cottage

chimney cap

split wood shingles

gambrel roof

gable

wood gutter

clapboards (weather-boarding)

end (corner) post

paneled door

nine-over-nine double-hung sash

The Cape Cod cottage originated with English settlers in the mid-1600s; although it is associated with the early Colonial period, the type actually prevailed well into the 1800s. The basic form consisted of a one- or two-room house with a loft above and, often, a lean-to at the rear. Sometimes a third room was added at the end. A pitched, bowed, or gambrel roof sloped down just to the window tops.

Built low and broad to withstand prevailing winds, the shingled or clapboard Cape Cod cottage often sat directly on timber sills without a foundation. If the sandy soil underneath eroded or blew away, the house could be dragged or floated to a new location.

hall/kitchen

parlor

Connected Farm

shingle siding — shed roof

rubblework foundation — barn — hanging sliders — back house (shed and storage)

privy — summer kitchen

shed and storage

kitchen

hay mow

woodshed

parlor — parlor

vehicle storage

tie-up

split wood shingles

pitched roof

gable

eaves

two-over-two
double-hung
sash

sidelight

fascia
board

end (corner) post

wood sill

(boarding)

The connected farm—a rambling complex of attached houses, barns, and animal sheds—is indigenous to northern New England. The supplementary buildings were usually added one by one over time, often as frugal Yankee farmers moved older, obsolete outbuildings from elsewhere on their property closer to the main house for reuse.

While the frigid winters of the region might explain this folk type, connected farms were not common until the mid-1800s and never appeared in other regions of the country that get just as cold as the Northeast. Rather, the connected farm probably developed in response to economic needs. As the 19th century progressed, the poor New England soil couldn't support the more progressive, large-scale farming adopted elsewhere. In an effort to compete, New Englanders combined smaller-scale family farms with cottage industries, such as needlecrafts and canning, and adopted a convenient arrangement of buildings to serve agriculture and home industry under the same roof.

Cracker House

CABIN

split wood shingles

square-hewn logs (split boards nailed over cracks)

tie bar

projecting eaves

purlin   rafter

porch

kitchen

round logs

heart pine or cypress pier

corner board

stick-and-mud chimney

log joist

The term "Cracker" is thought to have originated in southern Georgia, where cracked corn was a dietary staple, but it also refers to the whip-cracking cattle drivers who made their way across the Florida border in the 1800s. Many so-called Cracker houses, found primarily in central Florida and the panhandle, were log cabins of the standard single- or double-pen, saddlebag, or dogtrot types (see pages 119–21) adapted to a semi-tropical climate. A large, cool porch invariably surrounded the house, which was raised off the damp ground on rot-resistant piers of cypress, heart pine, or limestone. Chimneys were made of sticks where stones were scarce, and the kitchen was often in a separate building.

The more substantial "four-square" house, of balloon frame construction, featured ample front and back porches and a hipped roof covered in tin to deflect sun. A cupola provided natural air conditioning; as warm air rose out of louvered vents, cool air was drawn in through open windows and doors.

kitchen

pen

porch   dogtrot   porch

pen

FOUR-SQUARE HOUSE

hipped roof — louvered vent

hipped roof (ribbed tin) —

cupola

fascia board

louvered vent

projecting eaves

two-over-two double-hung sash

plate glass

clapboards (weatherboarding)

porch

brick steps — sidelight — brick pier

porch

bedroom | bedroom

parlor | parlor

porch

Creole House

TOWN HOUSE

hipped roof

ridge course (barrel tiles)

entablature

cast-iron railing

vertical plank shutter

flat tiles

modillion course

fascia board

louvered shutter

balcony

transom

battens

French door (full-length casement)

cabinet

parlor

parlor

Once a common feature of the New Orleans streetscape during the 19th century, the Creole townhouse had a hipped or gabled roof and a one- or two-story gallery on both the front and the rear. The plan consisted of two large rooms; detached outbuildings served as the kitchen, washroom, and other work spaces. A typical construction technique consisted of vertical planks set directly onto the sill. These so-called flatboat boards were covered with horizontal weatherboarding, or clapboards.

The basic pavilion-roofed house of the French Colonial era (see page 52) evolved into a simple house that was common in Louisiana and on the Gulf Coast well into the 1800s. Called a Creole cottage (a Creole is a Louisiana native descended from French, Spanish, or West Indian settlers), or a *maison de maître*, its plan was a simple rectangle partitioned into two or four rooms (often all used for sleeping), usually with no interior halls. A rear stair in a cabinet (small room) sometimes led to rooms in a dormered attic. French doors opened onto a front gallery or directly onto the street. A secluded garden and a gallery, which both served as cool living spaces, were usually located behind the house.

Creole House

MAISON DE MAÎTRE

- pitched-roof dormer
- flat tiles
- pavilion roof
- ridge course (barrel tiles)
- clapboards (weatherboarding)
- corner board
- projecting eaves
- vertical plank shutter
- French door (full-length casement)
- brick foundation

CONSTRUCTION DETAIL

- clapboard
- flatboat board
- sill
- brick pier

bedroom	bedroom
bedroom	bedroom

Shotgun House

gable — pitched roof (ribbed tin)   clapboards

shed roof

exposed rafter

porch

porch

plate glass   brick pier   paneled door

two-over-two
double-hung sash

porch

porch

One room wide, the shotgun house featured a gable-end entry and consisted of two or three all-purpose rooms placed back to back. It was said that if a gun were fired through the front door, the shot would pass through all the rooms in a straight line and go right out the back door. A second story was often raised over the rear room.

Associated primarily with New Orleans, the Gulf Coast, and the rural South, the shotgun was used for workers' and tenants' housing, and by the 1920s was found as far afield as California and Chicago. The long, narrow house type is believed to have first come to America during the 19th century by way of free blacks migrating from Haiti to Louisiana, where it developed as an amalgam of African, French, and Arawak building traditions.

Conch House

TWO-STORY HOUSE

- pitched roof
- louvered vent
- gable
- cornice
- two-story gallery
- scroll-sawn gingerbread railing
- transom
- plate glass
- clapboards
- two-over-two double-hung sash
- louvered shutter
- brick pier

Natives of the West Indies—many immigrating to America to work in Florida's cigar industry—brought the Conch house to Miami and Key West in the late 19th century. (Native Bahamians were colloquially called "Conchs" at that time.)

This simple one- or two-story building form was raised on piers and featured a porch or two-story gallery, often decorated with gingerbread trim, to catch cool breezes. The earliest examples are said to have been crafted by ships' carpenters using a cross-braced timber system based on shipbuilding techniques, but the vast majority are actually balloon frame structures sheathed with clapboards.

ONE-STORY HOUSE

- pitched roof
- split wood shingles
- clapboards
- fascia board
- ribbed-tin shed roof
- cornice
- stone pier
- louvered shutter
- cement-over-stone foundation
- picket

Sod House

PITCHED-ROOF HOUSE

pitched roof

rafter tail

wood lintel

sod roof

wood lintel

sod wall

four-over-four double-hung sash

PPrevalent from the mid-1800s into the 1900s, the sod house, or "soddie," was a product of the Plains, where lumber and other building materials were scarce. A specially designed breaking, or "grasshopper," plow allowed settlers to cut furrows without turning over and destroying the soil, producing foot-wide blocks of sod known as "Kansas brick" or, more optimistically, "Nebraska marble." Blocks were laid with staggered joints, as bricks would be, with every third course (row) set crosswise and the chinks filled in with fine dirt; the interior might be plastered with clay. A twelve- by fourteen-foot house took about an acre of sod and a week to build. Although dirty and leak-prone, the sod, preferably tough buffalo grass, kept the interior warm in winter and cool in summer, withstood wind, and was also good, according to one early settler, for "stopping arrows and slowing bullets."

BARREL-ROOF HOUSE

barrel roof

lintel

sod

stone weight

rafter end

cross batten

two-over-two double-hung sash

SINGLE-PEN CABIN

Chimney plate, log rib, vertical planks, ridge pole, pitched roof, stick-and-mud chimney, knee, butting pole, eaves beam, ceiling joist, chimney prop, hewn-log firebox, round logs, mud-and-grass chinking, sill, log step, floor joist, pen

Although the Swedes were the first settlers to build log structures in America, the major tradition of log building here originated independently in the late 1600s to the early 1700s with German-speaking settlers (see pages 40–42) in the mid-Atlantic region. From Pennsylvania and Virginia, the tradition of log building began spreading south and west with migrating Germans and Scots-Irish in the 1730s and reached its height during the period of frontier expansion from the mid-18th to mid-19th centuries.

The basic log house form was the one-room, or single-pen, plan. The central-chimney "saddlebag" plan evolved when the single-pen house was enlarged by setting the gable end of a second log building against the chimney of the existing structure. An easier way to add on to a log house was to place a second cabin next to the first, gable to gable, and simply roof over the intervening space, producing the "dogtrot" (two pens and a passage) house. Pine and spruce were the preferred woods.

Log Building

SADDLEBAG CABIN

pitched roof

split wood shingles

rubblework chimney

gable

square-
hewn logs

vertical
plank door

stone step

gate

mud-and-grass
chinking

pen

pen

live-
stock
shelter

Log Building

DOGTROT CABIN

rubblework chimney

split wood shingles

loft

pitched roof

gable

eaves beam

ceiling joists

sill

six-over-six double-hung sash

dogtrot (pass-through)

mud-and-grass chinking

square-hewn logs

pen

dogtrot

pen

Log Building

NORDIC LOG HOUSE

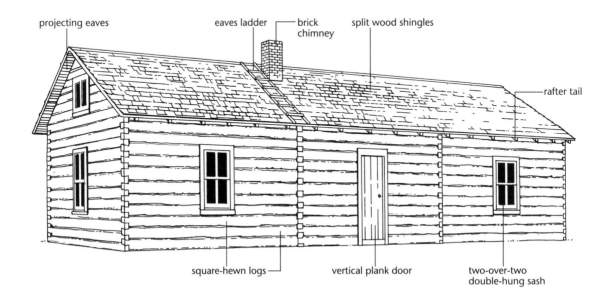

projecting eaves

eaves ladder — brick chimney

split wood shingles

rafter tail

square-hewn logs —

vertical plank door

two-over-two double-hung sash

parlor | kitchen | chamber

The square-hewn log house built by Nordic settlers, primarily in the upper Midwest, was characterized by a two-room plan, often with a third room added to make an I- or T-shaped layout. The door opened directly into the kitchen, an all-purpose room used for sleeping and daily work activities. The parlor was reserved for visitors.

Anatomy of Log Notching

SADDLE NOTCHES

V-NOTCH   **SQUARE NOTCH**   **DOVETAIL NOTCH**

STOVEWOOD CONSTRUCTION

Several different systems of corner notching were used in log construction. The saddle notch was employed universally for round logs, while various lapped (overlaid) and dovetail joints functioned best with squared logs. All logs were locked into place by their own weight. Joints were typically chinked with mud plaster or covered with narrow split boards. Stovewood log construction, found primarily in Wisconsin, involved embedding 8- to 10-inch-long log chunks, ends out, in limestone cement.

Fachwerk Building

FARMHOUSE (WISCONSIN)

pitched roof

split wood shingles

ceiling joist

wood lintel

rubblework chimney

transom light

clapboards

plate

shed roof

plate glass

two-over-two double-hung sash

vertical plank barn door

end (corner) post

cross brace

sill

transom

paneled door

post

fieldstone foundation

stucco-over-stone infill

A distinctive addition to the 19th-century frontier landscape of Wisconsin and Texas, where Germanic settlers homesteaded, was the small farmhouse built of *Fachwerk*, or half-timbering. *Fachwerk* consisted of a braced timber frame, usually of white oak or cedar, set on a squared timber sill over a fieldstone foundation. The open framework was filled with an insulation of mud and straw, sandstone, or nogging (kiln-fired brick). A coat of adobe or lime plaster was often applied over the walls, but the *Fachwerk* might also be left exposed.

Fachwerk Building

FARMHOUSE (TEXAS)

clapboards

ribbed-tin roof

brick chimney

shed roof

porch

paneled door

adobe plaster over sandstone infill

two-over-two double-hung sash

plate glass

beveled cedar post

gate

FRAMING DETAIL (HEWN CEDAR)

rafters

beam

queen posts

sandstone infill

post

cross brace

kitchen

bedroom

parlor

porch

Box-and-Strip Building

brick chimney

boxed eaves

split wood shingles (shakes)

shed roof

wood strips

rafter ends

vertical boards

porch

four-over-four double-hung sash

paneled door

wood pier

The simple box-and-strip construction technique appeared in the Plains and in Texas in the late 1800s after milled lumber became available but was still expensive in some hard-to-reach areas. Requiring a minimum of wood, the building method involved nailing vertical boards to a bottom sill and top plate, then merely covering up the cracks with thin wood strips. The look was similar to board-and-batten siding, but the strips were wider and rougher, and there was no balloon frame for support underneath.

kitchen

dining room

sitting room

bedroom

porch

Anatomy of a Balloon Frame

common rafters

collar beam

plate

second-floor joists

end joist

full-length stud

first-floor joists

sill

corner post (4x4)

masonry foundation

Invented in Chicago in the 1830s, the balloon frame consisted of slender individual, closely spaced studs extending the full height of the structure, whose members were nailed (with inexpensive, mass-produced nails), rather than mortised, together. Simple and light, it was far faster and cheaper to build than the post-and-beam frame and also required far less skill. The balloon frame had caught on widely by the mid-19th century and was used well into the 20th century, until modifications produced the platform frame (page 246).

Spanish Territorial Architecture

CASA DEL POBLADOR (TOWN HOUSE)

rafter tails (undressed logs bound with leather thongs)

shed roof

beam *(viga)*

whitewashed adobe plaster over adobe brick

casement

MISSION TILE DETAIL

After the Spanish Colonial period ended in 1821, a second generation of Spanish folk architecture developed in the Southwest and California territories, holding strong well into the 1900s. Beginning in the 1820s, wagon trains bearing Anglo settlers and goods from the East arrived along the Santa Fe Trail; later, with the railroads in the 1880s, factory-made window sashes, doors, gingerbread trim, and tin and shingle roofing materials traveled west. Adobe was still the basic building material, but wood clapboards appeared as commercial sawmills became common in the mid-1800s. Anglo and Spanish traditions melded; houses grew a story and gained porches and hipped and peaked roofs, producing a style sometimes known as "Monterey." Local craftsmen carved their own versions of factory-milled ornaments, yielding distinctive gates, window grilles, doors, and porch brackets.

Spanish Territorial Architecture

clay mission tiles

fascia board

grille

lattice railing

servants' dining room

fountain

dining room

kitchen

bed-room

loggia

path

loggia

bed-room

parlor

patio

bedroom

bench

gallery

bed-room

family chapel

passage

schoolroom

bed-room

street

Spanish Territorial Architecture

RANCHO

brick chimney

clapboards (weatherboarding)

pitched-roof dormer

double-pitched hipped pavilion roof

split wood shingles (shakes)

gallery

whitewashed adobe plaster over adobe bricks

beveled post

sidelight

six-over-six double-hung sash

gallery

MONTEREY-STYLE HOUSE

split cedar shingles

ridge course

hipped roof

plaster over brick chimney

two-story gallery

whitewashed adobe plaster over adobe brick

twelve-over-twelve double-hung sash

beveled post

gallery

Spanish Territorial Architecture

BARN

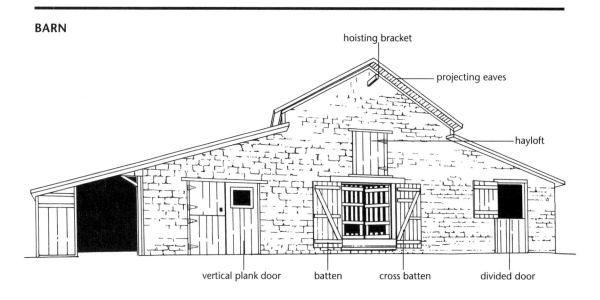

hoisting bracket

projecting eaves

hayloft

vertical plank door   batten   cross batten   divided door

ADOBE BRICK DETAIL

adobe bricks

adobe plaster

WINDOW GRILLES

top rail

stile

scroll-sawn spindle

bottom rail

top rail

stile

bottom rail

muntin

scroll-sawn spindle

scroll-sawn spindle

sill

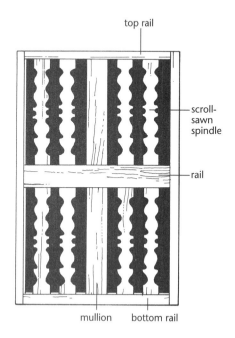

top rail

scroll-sawn spindle

rail

mullion

bottom rail

Chapter Seven
The Victorian Era

The Victorian era, which stretched from the 1830s to the turn of the century, was an age of great romanticism. Whereas the Renaissance-inspired interest in Classicism of the past century stressed intellect and reason, the Romantic movement appealed directly to the imagination, evoking mystery, passion, and nostalgia. Moody revivals of medieval European architecture came into fashion, and the ordered, sensible architecture of the Classical past fell out. Texture, color, and asymmetry replaced geometry and balance, and a broad range of lively, unconventional, and complex styles emerged.

The early Victorian styles, including the Gothic Revival and Italianate, were a direct reflection of the Picturesque, an aesthetic point of view celebrating the variety, texture, and irregularity inherent in nature. This resulted in a new and very strong interest in how a building related to its natural setting. Loggias, verandas, towers, and sleeping porches proliferated to take advantage of uplifting views and healthful fresh air, while asymmetrical floor plans designed to complement the natural site yielded wonderfully odd-shaped rooms.

As the century progressed, American architects continued to interpret and embellish European influences in their own ways, both looking to the inspiration of the past in the Queen Anne style and emulating current Parisian fashion with the Second Empire style. A fascination with decorative effect and material yielded the Stick and Shingle styles. And in an era of true eclecticism that fully embraced the eccentric, there was room not only for oddities such as the Octagon house, but also for the Adirondack style, the only Victorian building mode with entirely indigenous roots.

The Gothic Revival was the first of the Victorian-era styles to challenge the symmetry and ordered reason of Classicism. Brooding and romantic, it was a Picturesque mode, with vaulted ceilings, battlements, lancet-arch windows, and tracery all suggesting the mysterious architectural vocabulary of a distant past.

Popular in the 1830s and 1840s, the Gothic Revival was well suited to the dark brownstone increasingly used for the urban row house, but it was most commonly applied to the large country "villa" and to the small cottage, the first house type in America designed specifically for the middle class. The villa and cottage were introduced by the architect Alexander Jackson Davis (1803–92) in his 1837 volume *Rural Residences* and widely promoted by the influential landscape designer, Andrew Jackson Downing (1815–52), who also published several books. Widely used by the 1840s, the high-speed mechanical scroll saw, or jigsaw, allowed for the creation of exuberant gingerbread trim in wood, often found in what is called the Carpenter Gothic style.

ROW HOUSE

steeply pitched intersecting gable

chimney pot (can)

slate shingles

crenelated balcony

pinnacle

finial

coping

bargeboard (vergeboard or gable-board)

quatrefoil

hood molding (drip lintel)

lancet-arch casement

dripstone course

ashlar (squared building stone)

diamond-pane casement

three-sided oriel

pointed arch

corbeled oriel base

recessed entry

lancet-arch sidelight

stoop

downspout

Gothic Revival

VILLA (MASONRY)

pinnacle

battlement

slate shingles

stacked chimney

conical roof

stepped parapet

clustered chimney pots (cans)

triangular arch

shaped parapet

dripstone course

tower

label molding (square-arch hood molding)

cusped transom

pointed arch

cresting

ashlar (squared building stone)

recessed entry

diamond-pane casement

buttress

three-sided bay

BOSS DETAIL

RECEPTION HALL

rib

boss

ribbed vault

corbel stone

pointed arch

hood molding (drip lintel)

tracery

diamond-pane casement

faux stone (painted)

stone tile

baseboard

Gothic Revival

VILLA (CARPENTER GOTHIC)

finial

pinnacle

paired chimney pots (cans)

diamond-pane casement

ridge

steep pitched roof

boxed cornice

louvered shutter

jerkinhead (clipped gable)

bargeboard (vergeboard or gableboard)

steeply pitched intersecting gable

valley

trefoil plaque

projecting eaves

oriel

pendant (drop)

door hood

cresting

hood molding (drip lintel)

board-and-batten siding

pointed arch

bay   veranda   quatrefoil   transom   stop   tracery

braced arch (openwork truss)   arris   cusped arch

BOARD-AND-BATTEN DETAIL

battens

boards

washroom

bathing room

bed chamber

parlor

veranda

conservatory

kitchen

dining room

parlor

veranda

wood storage

porch

COTTAGE

bouquet finial

stacked chimney

cast-iron ridge cresting

pitched-roof dormer

diamond-patterned slate shingles

jerkinhead (clipped gable)

bargeboard (vergeboard or gableboard)

colored glass

pitched roof

projecting eaves

rafter tails

quatrefoil cornice trim (scroll-sawn wood)

skylight

triangular arch

diamond-pane casement

ashlar (squared building stone)

three-sided bay

quatrefoil panels

entry porch

lancet-arch casement

pointed-arch door panel

conservatory

kitchen

veranda

drawing room

library

dining room

porch

hall

Pattern Book Fences

The Model Architect (1852–53) by the popular 19th-century Philadelphia architect Samuel Sloan was an extremely successful Victorian-era pattern book, containing designs for many finishing details such as these fences. The top fence, claimed the author, was a fine specimen of rustic pattern, suitable for any ornamental villa. The center design ($1.50 per foot), made of cast iron, was best for a large building, while the last was intended as a "neat" pattern for a cottage or farmhouse.

TERRA-COTTA CHIMNEY POTS (CANS)

cap

cap

crenelated cap

herringbone-patterned shaft

lozenge-patterned shaft

spiral-patterned shaft

base

base

base

WINDOWS (EXTERIOR)

triangular arch

hood molding (drip lintel)

lozenge pane

label stop

casement

mullion

sill

apron

ogee arch

merlon

crenel

foil

crenelation

cusped arch

cusp

mullion

transom bar

tracery

oriel

sill

hood molding (drip lintel)

label stop

lancet arch

mullion

diamond pane

corbeled oriel base

Gothic Revival

COTTAGE (RUSTIC)

rustic wood cresting

chimney pot (can)

diamond-patterned slate shingles

pitched-roof dormer

bargeboard (vergeboard or gableboard)

hood molding (drip lintel)

pitched roof

rough-cast brick

rafter tails

ribbed-tin roof (painted in stripes)

rustic-work post and bracket

nine-over-six double-hung sash

veranda

sidelight

quatrefoil panel

water closet

pantry

laundry

closet

veranda

kitchen

library

passage

parlor

dining room

hall

veranda

Italianate

Well represented on the pages of pattern books, the Italianate style emerged in the 1830s along with the Gothic Revival and eventually proved more popular, lasting into the 1870s. With their square towers, asymmetrical plans, broad roofs, and generous verandas, the rambling Italianate houses that began to appear in both the suburbs and the countryside were rather free and highly romanticized interpretations of the villas of Tuscany, Umbria, and Lombardy. During the mid-1800s, the Italianate style was enthusiastically adapted for urban row house architecture and reached its zenith in the brownstone-fronted rows of New York, characterized by ornate door and window designs, weighty bracketed cornices, and high stoops with robust cast-iron stair rails.

PANELED DOUBLE DOORS (EXTERIOR)

roundel
hood molding (drip lintel)
corbel stone
pendant drop
colonnette
inset panel
door mullion

entablature
cornice
acanthus leaf frieze
egg-and-dart molding
inset panel
door mullion

Italianate

VILLA

chimney
fascia board
scroll-sawn brackets
tower
ribbed-tin shed roof
dripstone course
projecting eaves
hood (ribbed tin)
paired round-arch windows
rough-cast brick
balcony
veranda
beveled posts
paneled double door

kitchen
privy
pantry
dining room
drawing room
hall
drawing room
parlor
vestibule
veranda

CORNICE DETAIL (SECTION VIEW)

rafter
cornice
scroll-sawn bracket
fascia board

ROW HOUSE

fascia board

cornice

modillion course

foliate bracket

foliate bracket

two-over-two double-hung sash

bracket

sill

segmented-arch window

ashlar (squared building stone)

stone lintel (segmented)

segmented pediment

modillion course

plate glass

foliate keystone

round-arch transom

foliate bracket

paneled double door

one-over-one double-hung sash

louvered shutter

baluster

cast-iron railing

bannister

rusticated stone

newel cap

recessed joint

stoop

cast-iron grille (window guard)

Octagon

nine-over-nine double-hung sash

cupola

scroll-sawn bracket

louvered shutter

ribbed-tin roof

modillion course

fascia board

stucco

cornice

veranda

Doric column

lattice vent

sidelight

French door (full-length casement)

I n 1848, Orson Fowler (1809–87)—an extraordinary self-styled Renaissance man who made a living as a phrenologist, sex educator, and marriage counselor—published a wildly successful architectural handbook. Meant to bring "comfortable dwellings within the reach of the poorer classes," *A Home for All* introduced plans for the eight-sided house. Dismissing the square plan as woefully outdated, Fowler felt the Octagon plan made better use of a square or rectangular space because a wall of the same perimeter could enclose some 20 percent more floor area. Promoting comfort and convenience, he also advocated the use of central heating, dumbwaiters, speaking tubes, and indoor water closets. The fad for Octagon building faded with the financial panic of 1857, but by then thousands of Octagon homes, as well as Octagon barns, pig sties, and even a few seance chambers, had already been built.

living room

bedroom

dining room

parlor

hall

veranda

closet

BARN

louvered vent
cupola
wood shingles
vertical plank siding
hayloft
strap hinge
herringbone-patterned door
ramp
rafter tails
shed roof
hanging slider
diagonal plank door
six-over-six double-hung sash
rubblework foundation

harness room
oat bin
box stall
wagon storage
manure shed
trough
stall

Second Empire

pitched-roof dormer

hexagonal-shaped slate shingles

bracketed finial

pedimented dormer (segmented)

cast-iron cresting

scroll-sawn bracket

tower

hood

mansard roof

balcony

paired scroll-sawn brackets

scroll-sawn spandrel

veranda

two-over-two double-hung sash

three-sided bay

lancet-arch window

plate glass

clapboards

stoop

newel

entry porch

The Second Empire style took its inspiration directly from the skyline of Paris, which had been dramatically overhauled under the reign of Napoleon III during France's Second Empire period (1852–70). Two well-attended Paris exhibitions in 1855 and 1867 attracted enormous attention to the grandiose style, which found its first expression in public and civic buildings in America in the 1850s. It was particularly favored during the boom period following the Civil War under the administration of Ulysses S. Grant (1869–77). The signature mansard roof—which made good used of attic space—prominent cornices, ornate cresting, projecting pavilion fronts, and round dormers were adopted for splendid private homes and row houses across the country. The style began to fade by 1880.

Second Empire

CAST-IRON CRESTING

SLATE SHINGLES

STABLE

weathervane

cupola

louvered vent

diamond-shaped slate shingles

pedimented dormer

mansard roof

hayloft

paired scroll-sawn brackets

clapboards

two-over-two double-hung sash

Stick Style

SEASIDE ESTATE

weathervane

colored-glass transom

cast-iron cresting

steep pitched-roof gable

strut

jerkinhead (clipped gable)

porte cochère

applied stickwork

plate glass

clapboards

split wood shingles

jerkinhead (clipped gable)

scroll-sawn bracket

scroll-sawn spandrel

one-over-one double-hung sash

wood shingles

veranda

brick foundation

braced arch (openwork truss)

The highly picturesque Stick style, which is thought to have developed as a resort architecture, was richly expressed in several houses designed by Richard Morris Hunt (1827–95) in Newport, Rhode Island. Hunt was one of many American architects influenced by a mid–19th-century European revival of late-medieval rustic country architecture, most notably the gingerbread-ornamented chalets of the Alps and the half-timbered cottages of Normandy and Tudor England. The revival spread to America largely by way of several widely circulated German architectural journals.

The charm of the Stick style was impossible to resist, with its bright, contrasting paint colors, ornamental brackets and bargeboards, lacy openwork balconies, overhanging eaves, colored shingles, and the purely decorative criss-cross timbers, or stickwork, for which the style was later named (in the mid-1900s). By the 1860s, marvelously elaborate Stick style confections were appearing across the country, and the style remained popular in resorts, suburbs, and small towns well into the 1870s.

Stick Style

COTTAGE

chimney viewer

applied truss

king post

collar beam

strut

pendant (drop)

corbeled bracket

plate glass

sawtooth siding

projecting eaves

strut

split wood shingles

shed roof

beveled strut

two-over-two double-hung sash

veranda

clapboards

scroll-sawn railing

brick foundation

lattice vent

paneled door

Stick Style

PARLOR

coffer

paired modillion brackets

cornice

scroll-sawn bracket

colored-glass inset

bull's eye

plate glass

stenciled pattern

brick masonry

patterned brick

overmantel

mantel

ceramic-tile inset

round arch

voussoirs

checkerboard-pattern wood stain

fender

firebox

ceramic-tile hearth

oak board floor

Stick Style

SEASIDE COTTAGE

- tower
- colored hexagonal shingles
- mansard roof
- sawtooth shingles
- finial
- projecting eaves
- scroll-sawn spandrel
- braced arch (openwork truss)
- vertical siding
- wood cresting
- shed roof
- strut
- incised lintel
- plate glass
- one-over-one double-hung sash
- terrace
- scroll-sawn railing
- lattice vent

kitchen

entry

dining room

parlor

terrace

Queen Anne

ROW HOUSE

modillion course

front-facing gable

molded plaster decoration

finial

pediment

lozenge-shaped light

clapboards

foliate modillion

fascia board

foliate bracket

Ionic colonnette

broken pediment

cartouche

foliate keystone

rusticated stone

bell roof

imbricated shingles

turret

one-over-one double-hung sash

plate glass

decorative oriel base

Ionic column

recessed entry

recessed joint

carriage house

high stone stoop

Among the attractions generating considerable interest at the 1876 Centennial Exhibition in Philadelphia were several English buildings designed in the Queen Anne style, which would be widely influential in America from the 1870s until the turn of the century. The style was identified with the Scottish-born architect Richard Norman Shaw (1831–1912) and his followers, whose domestic work in England was a tremendously free and eclectic hybrid of forms drawn from a range of sources, including Classical, Tudor, and Flemish architecture.

Queen Anne style dismissed the impractical Gothic by emphasizing human scale and domestic comfort. Its facades showed a great variety, featuring projecting oriels, bay win-

ROW HOUSE

dows, and odd roof-lines. It was also rich in texture, with cut and molded brick, terra-cotta, and ornamental plaster. The open, asymmetrical plan centered around a "great hall" with an enormous fireplace and homey built-in inglenooks.

In America, the style found an exuberant expression in wood, and frequently incorporated Classical columns and decorative motifs borrowed from our own Colonial architecture. The Queen Anne style was favored for everything from row houses to sprawling seaside retreats, whose designs frequently came from pattern books. All were resplendent in patterned shingles, spindles, brackets, and curlicue cutouts; many boasted ample verandas, turrets, and sleeping porches.

flared chimney
sunflower finial
stone cresting
hipped-roof dormer
stone coping
slate shingles
swag frieze
sloping roof
baluster
stone balustrade
decorative hung tile
colored glass inset
transom
oriel
semicircular oriel
decorative oriel base
rowlock arch
multipane transom
imbricated shingles
recessed balcony
corbeled chimney base
rubblework masonry
swan's neck pediment
cast-iron cresting
multipane sash
paneled divided door
paneled gate
cast-iron vent

Queen Anne

ROW HOUSE

projecting eaves

paneled fascia boards

flat roof

coping

incised scroll-sawn bracket

soffit

incised decoration

dogtooth pattern

beaded board siding

beveled sash

plate glass

sunburst pediment

balcony

bracketed cornice

arched transom

multipane window

one-over-one double-hung sash

eared (crossetted) panel

stone stoop

masonry foundation

carved panel

squared bay

DRAWING ROOM

coffers — boxed beam

imbrication — carved griffin

pointed arch — crenelated cornice

stenciled border

pinnacle

curtain rod

raised (fielded) panels

hood

mantel

wainscot

dwarf column   firebox   herringbone-patterned border

Queen Anne

SEASIDE ESTATE

patterned ridge
weathervane
imbricated shingles
carved sunburst
corbeled chimney cap
steeply pitched gable
multi-pane sash
ribbed chimney
triple windows
turret
wood shingles
hipped roof
angled porches
veranda
turned post
plate glass
pendant (drop)
one-over-one double-hung sash
clapboards

butler's pantry
kitchen
storage
veranda
dining room
great hall
pocket doors
reception hall
veranda
parlor
porch

SEASIDE COTTAGE

pinnacle

finial

round-arch window

front-facing gable

truncated arched window

pitched roof

fascia board

cornice

scroll-sawn cornice trim

cornice

scroll-sawn spandrel

foliate lintel

sawtooth border

clapboards

beveled post

end post

scroll-sawn railing

bracket

plate glass

arched panel (inset)

two-over-two double-hung sash

turned knob

newel post

louvered shutter

Queen Anne

STAIRS

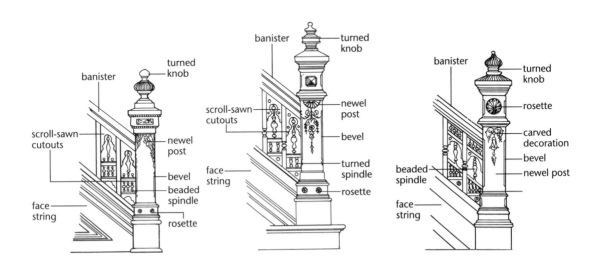

Queen Anne

INTERIOR FEATURES

DOUBLE DOORS

- incised cornice
- bull's eye
- guttae
- raised (fielded) panel
- paneled stile
- incised decoration
- beveled panel

ONE-OVER-ONE DOUBLE-HUNG SASH

- rosette
- upper sash
- lower sash
- plate glass
- paneled stile
- inset panel
- incised decoration

EXTERIOR FEATURES

THREE-SIDED BAY

- balustrade
- bracketed cornice
- dogtooth pattern
- turned knob
- beveled post
- shed roof
- scroll-sawn bracket
- multipane sash
- bull's eyes

SQUARED BAY

- sunburst
- beveled post
- hood
- scroll-sawn bracket
- multipane sash
- imbricated shingles

Queen Anne

BARGEBOARDS

SEASIDE ESTATE

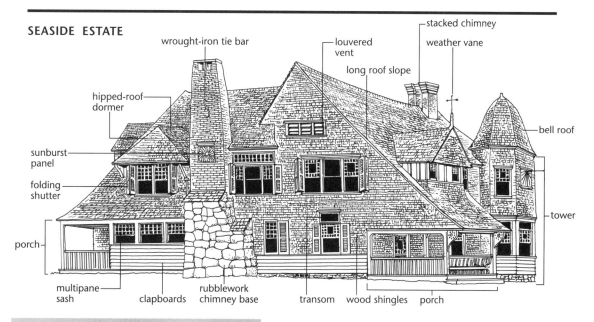

wrought-iron tie bar
stacked chimney
weather vane
louvered vent
long roof slope
hipped-roof dormer
bell roof
sunburst panel
folding shutter
porch
tower
multipane sash
clapboards
rubblework chimney base
transom
wood shingles
porch

The Shingle style had its genesis in the Boston area in the early 1880s. Over the next two decades it spread across the country, although it was favored for the rambling seaside estates and resorts of the New England coast. Like the Queen Anne style, the Shingle style was influenced by the work of the architect Richard Norman Shaw. This is especially evident in the innovative free-flowing plan, with large rooms and porches loosely arranged around an open "great hall," dominated by a grand staircase. On the exterior—stripped of excess decoration—shingles form a continuous covering, stretched smooth over roof lines and around corners in a kind of contoured envelope.

Henry Hobson Richardson (1836–86) is credited with developing the style and used it for most of his country and suburban houses, as did many prominent architects. The firm of McKim, Mead and White is also closely associated with the Shingle style; the partners often incorporated Colonial Revival motifs.

shed
pantry
dining room
parlor
kitchen
bath
great hall
porch
porch

Shingle Style

COUNTRY HOUSE

intersecting gable

pitched roof

shed-roofed dormer

louvered shutter

diamond-pane casement

rubblework chimney

waved shingles

eyebrow

hipped-roof dormer

boxed cornice

multi-level eaves

six-over-one double-hung sash

wood shingles

bargeboard (vergeboard or gableboard)

scroll-sawn rafter tails

veranda

lattice

pergola

cutout bracket

rubblework foundation

lozenge-shape lights

overhang

three-sided bay

porch

porch

china closet

pantry

kitchen

dining room

pergola

veranda

great hall

living room

porch

STABLE

hip-roofed dormer

flare

rubblework found

GREAT HALL

bull's eye — bracket — boxed beam — wallpaper border — cornice

wainscot

stenciled border

wainscot

fireplace

inglenook

stained wood

stair landing — hardwood floor — stained floor border

shed roof — brick chimney — splayed bracket — jerkinhead dormer — conical roof

recessed balcony

pitched roof

banded shingles

tower — grouped casements — wood shingles — tower

Romanesque Revival

The robust masonry forms and rich texture of this romantic style derive from the medieval Romanesque architecture of France and Spain. The characteristic features of the Romanesque Revival, including heavy rough-cut stone, round arches, squat dwarf columns, deeply recessed windows, and densely carved decoration with interlaced motifs, were imaginatively interpreted in massive freestanding houses and substantial row houses.

The architect Henry Hobson Richardson developed the style in the Boston area in the 1870s, and a monograph of his work published soon after his death in 1886 had a major influence throughout the country. Constructed of solid masonry, Romanesque Revival houses were expensive and, with the exception of row houses built on speculation, largely the purview of architects designing for affluent clients. The style was popular in urban and suburban areas. Interest in it faded in the 1890s.

DOUBLE ROW HOUSE

- red clay barrel tiles
- ridge tiles
- crocket
- hexagonal roof
- carved stone plaque
- tower
- diaper (allover pattern of repeating motifs)
- rough-cut brownstone masonry
- arch surround
- round arch
- cushion capital
- stone mullion

...secting gable

roundel

cornice return

hexagonal shingles

pitched-roof dormer

finial

modillion course

belt courses

flat (gauged) arch

multipane sash

brick masonry

voussoirs

colored-glass transom

plate glass

splayed stoop

f column aged)

round-arch transom

stone transom bar

Romanesque Revival

URBAN HOUSE

porch

pantry

kitchen

butler's pantry

pantry

veranda

china closet

servants' hall

dining room

chamber

private stairs

inglenooks

great hall

porte cochère

drawing room

library

reception

veranda

finial

hexagonal roof

colored glass transom

eyebrow

voussoir

shaped parapet

stacked chimney

multipane sash

dogtooth cornice

dwarf column

rough-cut stone lintel

mascaron (mask)

stone transom bar

stone mullion

merlon

crenel

recessed one-over-one double-hung sash

battlement

rinceau (band of curving plant motifs)

rough-cut brownstone

porte cochère

round arch

tower

veranda

paired columns

curved bay

STABLE

finial

ornamental gable

diamond-pane sash

louvered vent

pitched-roof dormer

hipped-roof dormer

dormer cheek

eyebrow

stone belt course

dogtooth

Syrian arch (springs from ground level)

coping

recessed entry

multipane sash

cowshed

carriage wash-room

stall

carriage room

harness room

Adirondack

While America's high-society industrialists and capitalists were lavishing millions on the palaces of Newport and other resorts, they also had a taste for "roughing it" in the wilderness. The result was the Great Camp of the Adirondack Mountains in northern New York State. Set up for extended summer stays, these sprawling complexes, and similar ones that appeared in other mountain regions of the country, included elaborate boathouses, guest quarters, kitchens, laundry and dining buildings, and hot running water. The look, however, was rustic, achieved with stone, logs, and twigs used in their natural state.

GREAT CAMP

decorative half-timbering · bracket · intersecting gable · steep sloping roof · ribbed-tin roof

exposed rafter

log siding

balcony

rubblework foundation

rough-pole porch post · paired windows

Adirondack

While they were usually built by local woodsmen, the camps were invariably designed by society architects; several were also the work of William West Durant, a New York State speculator who was credited with originating the Great Camp. For families of more modest means, many of the popular periodicals and handbooks of the day offered plans for woodland cabins that could be built for a few hundred dollars. The heyday of this rustic style lasted from the 1870s to the onset of the Depression.

ed-roofed dormer   split shingles   shed roof   stucco

scroll-sawn rafter tail

corbeled log ends

six-over-six double-hung sash

recessed porch   saddle notch   rubblework chimney   rustic-work railing (rough twigs)

A Rustic Dog Kennel

Dog Kennels
Jocks Lake Herkimer
McDutton Barber Owner

The camp style of architecture was a wholehearted celebration of the joys of nature. As a result, the rustic approach to decoration and design influenced every structure in a camp complex—even dog kennels like this one, pictured in the 1889 edition of *Log Cabins and Cottages: How to Build and Furnish Them* by William S. Wicks. The inherent picturesque quality of log construction was a big draw. Log cabins and outbuildings were closely associated with the nation's frontier heroes of the 19th century, suggesting—according to one contemporary periodical—"a certain glamor of romance."

BOATHOUSE

rubblework chimney

eyebrow

split shingles

split-log
roof sheathing

six-over-one
double-hung
sash

rustic
bracket

rustic-work
railing
(rough twigs)

balcony

rough-pole
porch post

boat entry

vertical log siding

twig decoration

dock

inglenook

living room/study

balcony

window seat

Adirondack

LIVING ROOM

exposed rough log beam

brick overmantel

log mantel

vertical plank door

paired windows

log siding

rough-pole mantel support

flat (gauged) arch

CABIN

pantry

kitchen

dining room

living room

porch

hipped roof

paired windows

shed roof

exposed log rafters

casement

rough-pole beam

log siding

split shingles

rubblework chimney

diamond-pane casement

saddle notch

rough-pole porch post

Victorian Fireplaces

overmantel mirror · overmantel

sawtooth border

mantel

bracket

polychromed pattern

colonette

bull's eye · firebox · tile facing

wood molding · hood

dwarf column

mantel

dentil course

inset panel

firebox

marble mantel · quatrefoils

marble tracery

cusps

marble colonette

firebox

wood molding

mantel

guilloche molding

corbeled bracket (bricks)

segmented arch

firebox

Victorian-era fireplaces typically featured ornate designs of brick or carved wood or stone. The example above is distinctly gothic; the others shown here might have been used interchangeably in a range of house styles.

Chapter Eight
Classicism and the Revivals

As the Victorian era waned, there emerged a new current in American architecture that consciously rejected the Picturesque. This "Academic Reaction," led by the influential New York firm of McKim, Mead and White, marked a return to formal, disciplined order and the kind of literal, archaeological adaptation of historical styles that had gone out with the Greek Revival. Rooted in a broader cultural movement then known as the American Renaissance, the renewed interest in historical European design (especially Classical and Renaissance forms), as well as a new interest in America's own Colonial past, could be seen in the overwhelming response to the Classically inspired design of the 1893 World's Columbian Exposition in Chicago. Equally influential were the principles of the Ecole des Beaux-Arts in Paris, which emphasized "correct" interpretations of historic architecture. While bookish and programmatic, the style known as Beaux Arts made up for its lack of spontaneity with an architecture outstanding for its balance and clarity, reasoned solutions to spatial and circulation problems, and true sense of grandeur, permanence, and "good taste."

With the 20th century came a related interest in a variety of period styles. Safe and conservative designs—based, for example, on the half-timbered manor houses of Tudor England and the country estates of Normandy and Spain—attracted the well-heeled clients who provided the bulk of business for the prestigious architectural firms of the day. While it took some time, the influence of these popular period revivals eventually spread to more modest suburban residences and was widespread by the 1940s, lasting into the present.

CHERUB (PUTTO)

CORBEL STONE

**GARGOYLE
(WATERSPOUT)**

Popularized in the 1880s by the fashionable society architect Richard Morris Hunt (1827–95), the Chateauesque was perhaps the most grandiose of the late Victorian styles, epitomizing all the excesses of the Gilded Age. The Chateauesque was loosely based on the 15th- and 16th-century French chateaux of the Loire Valley. The American versions, built primarily in New York and other eastern cities, were in fact modified stone castles, complete with steeply pitched hipped roofs, elaborate dormers and gable parapets, towers, spires, and all manner of florid Gothic detailing, from gargoyles to griffins. Not to be outdone, the interiors boasted enormous reception halls, picture galleries, and conservatories, along with the latest in technological innovations, including electric passenger elevators and central steam heating. The style was fashionable into the first decade of the 1900s.

Chateauesque

URBAN HOUSE

finial — stacked chimney cap

parapet

parapet balcony

dormer

steeply pitched roof

conical roof

griffin

turret

gargoyle

pinnacle

corbel stone

limestone ashlar (squared building stone)

carved lime-stone balcony

arched transom

semi-circular bay

oriel

dripstone course

corbeled oriel base

transom

plate glass

belt course

pendant (drop)

semi-circular bay

corbel stones

Italian Renaissance

URBAN HOUSE

- parapet
- flat roof
- modillion course
- pediment
- cornice
- egg-and-dart moldings
- dripstone course
- segmented pediment
- inset panel
- two-over-two sash
- rosette frieze
- projecting lintel
- plate glass
- pulvinated frieze
- casement
- wrought-iron balustrade
- cartouche
- urn
- pedestal
- scallop
- niche
- recessed joint
- fret (meander or Greek key)
- flat (gauged) arch
- wrought-iron grille
- rusticated limestone
- embossed bronze door

The Italian Renaissance revival, directly inspired by the great Renaissance houses of Italy, was one of the most popular of the Beaux Arts design modes, lasting from the late 1800s until the 1920s. While the Victorian Italianate (pages 143–45) was essentially a loose interpretation of Italian architecture, drawn primarily from pattern books, the Italian Renaissance revival took a much more academic approach, with design features often copied directly from actual Renaissance landmarks. Roman, Florentine, and Venetian prototypes—ducal palazzi or country villas—were translated into American "palaces," primarily in cities such as New York and fashionable resorts like Newport, Rhode Island.

FIRST FLOOR

- scullery
- kitchen
- servants' hall
- hall
- butler's pantry
- main hall
- lavatory
- reception
- den
- vestibule

SECOND FLOOR

- service
- dining room
- hall
- library
- drawing room

Italian Renaissance

URBAN HOUSE

plate glass
keystone
limestone balustrade
roundel
corbeled chimney
hipped roof (ribbed copper)

balustrade
garland frieze
round-arched transom
Corinthian column (engaged)
entablature
carved spandrel
Ionic column (engaged)
modillion course
flat (gauged) arch
portico
rusticated limestone

recessed joint — casement — wrought-iron grille

dining room
breakfast room
hall
study
lavatory
secretary's office
music room
stair hall
salon
cloakroom
men's retiring room — vestibule

butler's pantry
safe
elevator
housekeeper's office
light well

Italian Renaissance

ROW HOUSE

modillions · oval window · Palladian window · garland-and-wreath frieze

cast-iron cornice

pediment

limestone masonry

paired arched windows

pediment

foliate bracket

one-over-one double-hung sash

rusticated window surround

wreath

Corinthian column (engaged)

plate glass

cartouche

balcony

foliate bracket

wrought-iron grille

stoop

Italian Renaissance

SUBURBAN HOUSE

hip-roofed dormer

clapboards

red clay barrel tiles

hipped roof

soffit

projecting eaves

gutter

paired brackets (corbeled)

stucco

six-over-one double-hung sash

downspout

corbeled capital

dripstone course

portico

planter box

semicircular bay

French door (full-length casement)

trellis

piers

GARAGE (AUTO BARN)

keystone

wood shingles

arched multipane doors

pediment

hipped roof

fascia board

pediment

entablature

squared columns

rubblework masonry

ROW HOUSE

Broadly speaking, the term "Beaux Arts" refers to the American Renaissance period from about 1885 to the 1920s and encompasses the Italian Renaissance and Neoclassical revivals. It is also used specifically to describe buildings derivative of contemporary work in France, based on Baroque architecture. In America, the Beaux Arts style was interpreted in imposing row and freestanding town houses as well as grandiose country estates. Characteristically, these impressive residences featured facades of pristine white limestone or elegant buff-colored or yellow brick in a narrow gauge, often accented with enormous cartouches dripping with sculptural ornament.

inset panel
modillion course
balusters
parapet
cartouche
limestone balustrade
cornice
foliate bracket
one-over-one double-hung sash
cornice
cartouche
plate glass
wrought-iron railing
leaded-glass transom
oriel
Roman brick (narrow gauge)
terminal figure
corbeled oriel base
recessed joint
rusticated limestone
wrought-iron fence
Corinthian column (engaged)
wrought-iron grille

Beaux Arts

ENTRANCE HALL AND GRAND STAIRCASE

mascaron (mask)

spandrel

decorated beam casing

marble pilaster

soffit

plaster medallion

arch

lantern

impost block (supports arch)

plaster molding

leaded-glass round-arched transom

paired marble columns

marble face string

wrought-iron grille

base

plinth

marble baseboard

marble tiles

wrought-iron railing

URBAN HOUSE

shingles

mansard roof

broken pediment (segmented)

ridge

crockets

cornice

foliate bracket

rounded corner

valley

one-over-one double-hung sash

pedimented dormer

modillion course

paired foliate brackets

cornice

balcony

transom

arched transom

limestone balustrade

French door (full-length casement)

band course

rusticated limestone

recessed joints

cherub (putto)

paneled door

recessed entry

wrought-iron grille

Neoclassical

ESTATE HOUSE

modillion course

parapet

projecting lintel

The Neoclassical revival was based on the Neoclassical architecture of 18th-century France and England. In America, fashion favored the French Neoclassical, which provided a striking alternative to the ostentatious sculptural ornament associated with the Beaux Arts style. By contrast, the flat-roofed Neoclassical house was subdued and dignified, although equally monumental in scale. Facades were markedly symmetrical, gaining interest from a deliberate play of clear glass against solid expanses of stone, and punctuated by rhythmic rows of columns, windows, and French doors. A grand two-story portico often emphasized the centrality of the design.

lavatory — coat closet

salon

living room

organ

hall

pantry

dining room

salon

writing room

reception room — entry

balusters

limestone balustrade

entablature

limestone

eared (crossetted) surround

Corinthian portico

grouped casements

French door
(full-length casement)

LIVING ROOM DETAIL

molded plaster cornice

plaster molding

urn

molded relief

swag

cornice

fielded (raised) panels

French door
(full-length casement)

wood wainscot

Colonial Revival

Following on the heels of America's Centennial celebrations, the Colonial Revival emerged in the early 1880s. The style, which borrowed heavily from early American architecture—particularly Georgian and Federal buildings—was largely an outgrowth of a new pride in America's past and a rapidly growing interest in historic preservation. Among the leaders of the movement were the partners at McKim, Mead and White, who had made a tour of New England's historic towns in 1878.

In this early phase, the Colonial Revival style remained the exclusive domain of fashionable architectural firms and was favored for the large residences of wealthy clients. Designs incorporated characteristic features of Colonial buildings, including Palladian windows, gambrel roofs, pedimented porticos, columns, Classical detailing such as swags and urns, and crisp white trim. The new buildings, however, were much larger than their historic counterparts, with the details also enlarged and plans laid out on a grandiose scale.

ROW HOUSE

Chinese Chippendale railing

pitched roof

coping

pedimented dormer

parapet

cornice

cornice bracket

voussoirs

six-over-six double-hung sash

brick masonry (Flemish bond)

splayed lintel

louvered shutter

wrought-iron balcony

entablature

Ionic column

portico

rusticated limestone

recessed joint

brick relieving (segmented) arch

wrought-iron gate

water table

wrought-iron grille

FREESTANDING STAIRCASE

GRAND STAIRCASE

FIREPLACES

balusters

paneled face string

banister

spindle

tread

riser

lip

keystone

leaded glass

chair rail

banister

lip

paneled wainscot

Doric pilaster

riser

tread

mantel   fan   ellipse   dentil course

entablature

colonette

marble facing

firebox   hearth

gougework   swag (garland)

mantel

colonette

inset panel

marble facing

fireback

hearth   firebox

Colonial Revival

ESTATE HOUSES

hipped roofs

pedimented dormer

swan's neck pediment

modillion course

wood shingles

limestone balustrades

semi-circular veranda

limestone quoin

balcony

semicircular portico

globe finial

Corin column

bicycle room

lavatory

inglenook

music/sitting room

kitchen

pantry

laundry

servants' veranda

veranda

butler's pantry

great hall

drawing room

dining room

terrace

vestibule

conservatory

tte

Palladian
window

crenellated
chimney

lipped lintel

cornice

six-over-six
double-hung sash

veranda

bblework terrace

brick masonry

turned balusters

gambrel roof

intersecting
gable

hip-roofed
dormer

wood shingles

eight-over-
one double-
hung sash

plate
glass

por-
tico

paired columns

awning (rolled up)

casements

fieldstone (schist) masonry

three-sided bay

French door
(full-length
casement)

Colonial Revival

Labels (top illustration):
pitched roof · swan's neck pediment · hipped-roof dormer · gable · brick roundel · twelve-over-twelve double-hung sash · gallery · flanker (dependency) · semicircular oriel · hyphen · portico · twelve-over-twelve double-hung sash · flanker (dependency)

Labels (floor plan):
elevator · dining room · pantry · vestibule · kitchen · servants' dining room · schoolroom · flanker · hyphen · children's dining room · salon · entry · living room · hyphen · hyphen · sunroom · library · flanker

Labels (bottom illustration):
pitched roof · intersecting gable · wood shingles · pitched-roof dormer · paneled shutter · clapboards · overhang (jetty) · trellis · segmented pediment · eight-over-twelve double-hung sash

French Revival

SUBURBAN HOUSE

tie-rod

slate shingles

steep hipped pavilion roof

shed-roofed dormer

modillion course

casement

stucco

built-in garage

louvered shutter

nine-over-six double-hung sash

paneled door

forecourt

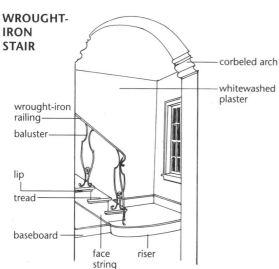

WROUGHT-IRON STAIR

corbeled arch

whitewashed plaster

wrought-iron railing

baluster

lip

tread

baseboard

face string

riser

The picturesque French Revival incorporated stylistic features from a broad period of French architecture spanning several centuries, but found its essence in the landed country estates of Brittany and Normandy. The most distinctive identifying features are the steeply pitched hipped pavilion roof, conical tower, and French doors. This popular style, lasting well into the 1940s, was used for high-style country estates and smaller suburban houses throughout America.

Classicism and the Revivals   193

French Revival

ESTATE HOUSE

steep hipped pavillion roof — round dormer — tall chimney

wood shingles

hipped-roof dormer

carved spandrel

garland swag

loggia

cornice

stucco over brick — urn — pedestal — wrought-iron balcony — louvered shutter — treillages

pantry/ servants' sitting room

hall

library

loggia

dining room

salon

living room

loggia

gravel terrace

marble terrace

STABLE

conical roof

rubblestone chimney

diamond shingle pattern

knees

weathervane

broken gable

half-timbering

cupola

wood shingles

pitched-roof dormer

diamond-pane casement

ribbon windows

rubblework masonry

nine-over-nine double-hung sash

porte cochère

tower

carriage room

stall room

harness room

carriage washroom

It was not unusual for a stable on a turn-of-the-century country estate to be larger than a typical suburban house. The main floor of this French-inspired design accommodated several carriages and horses; a second story contained rooms for male stable hands and house servants.

Spanish Revival

Spanish-inspired houses began appearing at the turn of the century in the form of the Mission style, which reflected a loose adaptation of features often found on Spanish Colonial mission buildings, including the shaped parapet and quatrefoil window. In 1915 the California-Pacific Exposition opened in San Diego to inaugurate the Panama Canal. One of the great stars of the fair was the California pavilion, a romantic, slightly exotic building designed in a freely interpreted Spanish Colonial style by the fashionable architect Bertram Grosvenor Goodhue (1869–1924). Both the exposition and Goodhue did much to promote this more academic and sophisticated interpretation, which borrowed from a broad vocabulary of Moorish, Byzantine, and Renaissance detailing, often based on actual prototypes in Spain. In vogue into the 1930s, the Spanish Revival was found primarily in the Southwest, California—where it was a style of choice for Hollywood stars—and fashionable Florida resorts.

ESTATE HOUSE

SUBURBAN HOUSE

molded plaster decoration

semicircular pediment

molded plaster relief

coping

decorative vent

ridge course

red clay mission tiles

hipped roof

wrought-iron tie-rod

shaped parapet

modillion course

leaded glass

downspout

cornice

hood molding

scroll bracket

arched transom

single-pane casement

plate glass

loggia

fluted column

fan

balustrade

transom

GARAGE (AUTO BARN)

coping

shaped parapet

red clay barrel tiles

projecting eaves

planter box

buttress pier

diagonal boards

Spanish Revival

STAIRCASE (INTERIOR)

DOOR (INTERIOR)

casement

twisted-
rope
handrail

white-
washed
stucco

embedded
ceramic tile

ceramic
face tile

clay floor tiles

hinge

wrought-
iron trim

drop latch

studs

**WROUGHT-IRON
STRAP HINGES**

PATIO

red clay barrel tiles

molded plaster relief

wrought-iron balcony

pergola

chimney

stucco over brick masonry

loggia

transom

herringbone-patterned brick

reflecting pool

slate tile

French door (full-length casement)

Tudor Revival

trefoil cutout — valley — stacked chimney — shed-roofed dormer — intersecting gable

pitched-roof dormer

bargeboard (vergeboard or gableboard)

half-timbering

balustrade

pointed arch — rubblework terrace — diamond-pane casement — rubblework masonry

The high-style Tudor Revival house of the late 19th and early 20th centuries derived primarily from English Renaissance buildings of the 16th and early 17th centuries, including those of the Elizabethan and Jacobean periods. These rambling, asymmetrically massed mansions typically featured steeply pitched roofs, one or more intersecting gables, decorative—rather than structural—half-timbering, and long rows of casement windows. By the early 20th century the Tudor Revival style was adapted to the middle-class suburban house and eventually became especially popular for the affordable small house of the 1920s and 1930s (page 212). There have been periodic revivals ever since.

GARAGE (AUTO BARN) — pitched roof — slate shingles — oak crossbeam

clapboards

decorative tail

lantern

leaded glass

stucco

vertical plank door (knotty oak) — wrought-iron strap hinge — half-timbering

tucco

pitched roof

wood shingles

knee

cross brace

ix-over-one
double-hung sash

**SUBURBAN
HOUSE**

chimney pot

quarter-round
lunette

knees

slate shingles

steeply pitched
sloping gable

leaded-glass
casement

clapboards

stucco

arched window

French door
(full-length casement)

end (corner)
post

girt

vertical plank door

storeroom

porch

dining
room

pantry

kitchen

loggia

hall

lobby

flagstone
porch

living room

Classicism and the Revivals 201

Chapter Nine
New American Visions

While period styles represented a major design current during the early 1900s, a few progressive minds began to establish influential standards of design wholly independent of historical European references. Among the strongest voices against the Classicism and formal composition of the Beaux Arts movement was that of Frank Lloyd Wright (1867–1959). Wright's work drew on many sources, including Japanese design, the contemporary English Arts and Crafts movement, and the Victorian preoccupation with the relationship of a building to its natural environment. Interpreted in the context of the flat Midwestern landscape—and Wright's own very personal design vocabulary—his Prairie style evolved as a truly original American art form.

The equally intelligent Craftsman designs of Charles Sumner Greene (1868–1957) and his brother Henry Mather Greene (1870–1954) were another important departure from the past. The fascination of these California architects with structural forms and the pure, simple beauty of wood and stone yielded superbly articulated buildings organically integrated with their sites.

Designed for an affluent clientele, the high-style Prairie and Craftsman houses had a relatively short life, over by the 1920s. But Wright and the Greene brothers were among the first American designers of their generation to emphasize comfort and convenience, and their concepts of human scale and sensible plans (alien to most Victorian architecture) helped shape a growing phenomenon of the time: the affordable small house for the middle class.

SUBURBAN HOUSE

clay tiles — hipped roof — horizontal chimney

soffit

stucco

built-in planter box

projecting eaves

one-over-one double-hung sash

inset wood banding

piers

porch

squared bay

The Prairie School designs of Frank Lloyd Wright and his followers embodied Wright's belief that a building should appear to grow organically from its site. In Wright's mind, a design drew its beauty from within—from its own anatomy—rather than from applied decoration. The Prairie house was deliberate and composed, conceived as a practical, cohesive whole down to the landscaping, built-in furniture, and fixtures, which were treated with as much importance as the architectural elements. Its natural textures and horizontal profile, accented by broad, hovering roof planes and spreading terraces, were in concert with the flat landscape of the midwestern plains. Inside, the simplified open plan had a minimum of rooms, defined by screens and panels, radiating from a central living space.

The Prairie house, which ranged from modest designs to huge estates, reached its peak in Oak Park, Illinois, and other Midwest suburbs during the first two decades of the 20th century. Client interest in the large-scale version had faded by World War I, but the open floor plan, clean lines, and human scale associated with the style made a permanent mark on American architecture, particularly small-scale suburban house design.

Prairie School

LARGE SUBURBAN HOUSE

cast-plaster decorative frieze

low-pitched roof

soffit

projecting eaves

dripstone course

colored-glass clerestory windows

pier

buttress pier

grouped casements (ribbon windows)

enclosed porch

pedestal urn

narrow voussoirs

pier

round arch

built-in planter box

horizontal chimney

clay tiles

projecting gable peak

copper fascia

Roman brick (narrow gauge)

porch

...rete water table

elevator

cold storage

butler's pantry

breakfast nook

kitchen

dining room

terrace

porch

parlor

living room

porch

servants' dining room

garden entry

reception hall

service kitchen

alcove

gallery

conservatory

enclosed porch

bath

bedroom

entry hall

terrace

dressing room

porch

Prairie School

**SUBURBAN
HOUSE**

hipped-roof dormer

hipped roof

clay tiles

stucco

soffit

grouped diamond-
pane casements

projecting
eaves

hipped-roof porch

clapboards

ribbed railing

paneled pier
(roof to ground)

rubblework foundation

GARAGE

split wood shingles

horizontal chimney

projecting eaves

diamond-
pane
pivoting
windows

inset
wood
banding

ribbed door

stucco

LIVING ROOM

plaster ceiling panels — stained walnut ribs

painted mural

curtained bookshelf

carpet

concrete mantel

wood floor border

Roman brick (narrow gauge) wainscot

WINDOWS

mullion

divider (copper electroplated with zinc)

colored glass

PAIRED CASEMENTS

mullion

dividers

colored glass

CLERESTORY WINDOW

colored glass

divider (copper electro-plated with zinc)

FIXED WINDOW

Craftsman

grouped casements (ribbon windows)

chimney cap

low-pitched roof

exposed beam

intersecting gable

projecting eaves

exposed rafters

beams

veranda

strut

queen post

brick and quarry stone

picture window

corbeled bracket

The Craftsman style represented an independent western movement in American architecture. Its guiding force was the English Arts and Crafts movement, which rejected the mass reproduction and mediocre design associated with the Industrial Revolution in favor of the beauty and "honesty" of traditional handcraftsmanship and natural materials.

In America these ideas were widely disseminated in the pages of the *Craftsman* magazine, published from 1901 to 1916 by the furniture maker and designer Gustav Stickley (1848–1942). The style was adapted for countless small houses and bungalows (see page 212) but found its most sophisticated expression in the California work of Pasadena architects Greene and Greene. Trained in the manual arts, these brothers were craftsmen who often became involved in the actual building of houses. Spanning the period of 1903 to 1928, their domestic work showed a love for material, technology, and craft—particularly the workmanship of Japanese architecture. Sheathed in dark shingles, the high-style Craftsman house was at one with its setting, the gardens and loggias treated as planned extensions of the architecture. Hand-polished woods such as oak, teak, and mahogany detailed each interior. Built-in features crafted of fine materials made each house a giant sculpture, with each detail part of the whole.

Craftsman

split wood shingles

three-sided bay

beam

joists

pier (roof to ground)

pergola

tone lantern

coping (rowlock course)

sloping (battered) foundation

porte cochère

pantry

garage

cold storage

dining room

kitchen

bed-room

courtyard

hall

bath

entry

bath

bed-room

bed-room

hall

hall

veranda

living room

entry

pergola

terrace

Craftsman

GARAGE

planter box — exposed purlins — exposed beams

corbeled tail

stucco

wood slats

built-in bench

brick foundation

herringbone-patterned brick drive

ribbed oak door

wrought-iron strap hinge

DOORS (INTERIOR)

top rail

top rail

top rail

colored glass

hanging stile

bowed rib

hand plate

shutting stile (touch-spring mechanism)

shutting stile

hanging stile

bottom rail

bottom rail

bottom rail

Craftsman

ENTRANCE HALL

colored-glass clerestory window

colored-glass copper lantern

beams

colored glass

ebony pegs

teak stairwall

stepped banister

BEAM DETAIL

tongue

wrought-iron strap

wedge

teak beam

tongue

ebony peg

Bungalows and Small Houses

CRAFTSMAN BUNGALOW

low-pitched roof
grouped windows
cutout bracket
split wood shingles
projecting eaves
rafter tails
kick
shed roof
plate glass
clapboards
squared bay
dwarf pier
eight-over-one double-hung sash

porch
ice box
kitchen
bedroom
closet
dining room
bath
linen closet
closets
living room
bedroom
porch

The first thirty years of the 1900s were a building boom for the small single- and two-family house, along with the detached "auto barn," or garage. This growth was spurred by a social movement to improve housing, as well as another development on the American scene: the suburb. In 1900 there were 8,000 cars on the road; just fifteen years later the number was well over two million. This automobility, along with improved railroads, created a demand for affordable housing within reach of the city.

Magazines led the way. Among the most influential was *Ladies Home Journal*, which around 1900 published designs for small model homes—often in chalet and period styles— complete plans for prefabricated frames, specifications for fireproofing, and such novel conveniences as electricity, plumbing, and gas ranges. The *Craftsman* (see page 208) was responsible for the widespread popularity of the Craftsman bungalow, a typically snug one-and-a-half-story home with a wide overhanging roof, deep porch, and simple interior with built-in cupboards and cozy inglenooks. For a few dollars a reader could purchase working plans for a house costing as little as $1,000 to build. Ready-to-build houses could also be bought by mail order from enterprises such as Sears, Roebuck, which would deliver the crated materials, fixtures, and assembly instructions for an entire house to the nearest railroad station.

CRAFTSMAN BUNGALOW

chimney pot (can)

split wood shingles

arched window

split wood shingles

nine-over-one double-hung sash

shed roof

rubblework masonry

sloping dormer

paired windows

sloping pitched roof

porch

brackets

squared oriel

plate glass

FIRST FLOOR

porch — pantry — porch

kitchen

dining room

inglenook

living room

hall

vestibule

porch

SECOND FLOOR

bedroom

bath

closets

linen closet

closet

bedroom

bedroom

Bungalows and Small Houses

"ENGLISH" HOUSE

double-pitched dormer

cross brace

decorative half-timbering

valley

slate shingles

intersecting gable

steep pitched roof

projecting eaves

six-over-six double-hung sash

flared eaves

stucco

recessed entry

"FARM" HOUSE

hipped-roof dormer

hipped roof

split wood shingles

one-over-one double-hung sash

projecting eaves

plate glass

fascia board

clapboards

porch

Anatomy of a Steel Frame

triangular unit

truss

channel
beams

triangular
unit

girt (formed
from hori-
zontal units

girt (formed
from hori-
zontal units

sill

vertical unit

vertical unit

angle studs

Designed as a safe, fire-resistant, economical, and "vermin-proof" alternative to wood, this flexible system of steel frame construction was introduced in a 1926 model house built in Tarrytown, New York. An early example of prefabrication, it consisted of various standard widths and heights. Each unit was punched with holes and could easily be bolted together once in place. A facing of brick, wood siding, stucco, or stone could be applied to the exterior; interior partitions were finished with plaster applied over wire lath.

Bungalows and Small Houses

"SPANISH" HOUSE

shaped parapet — flat roof — niche — inset tile — bracket — twisted (spiral) chimney cap — chimney

stucco — recessed casement — gate — twisted (spiral) colonette — French door (full-length casement)

"DUTCH" HOUSE

louvered vent — intersecting gables — valley

gambrel roof — projecting eaves

rafter tails — plate glass

kick

splayed column

one-over-one double-hung sash

clapboards

rubblework pier

Bungalows and Small Houses

CHALET

jerkinhead (clipped gable)

finial

split wood shingles

scalloped cornice trim

eyebrow dormer

exposed rafter

six-over-one double-hung sash

decorative cornice board

projecting eaves

scroll-sawn bracket

clapboards

grouped windows

plank shutter

trellis

decorative cutout

scroll-sawn railing

turned porch post

diamond-paneled door

stucco

rubblework masonry

CHALET GARAGE

exposed rafters

scroll-sawn bracket

stone roof weights

split wood shingles

scalloped cornice board

projecting eaves

decorative cutout

vertical plank shutter

herringbone-patterned door

ramp

cement foundation

Bungalows and Small Houses

TWO-FAMILY HOUSE

decorative vent · colored-slate shingles · broken gable

pitched roof

gutter

grouped windows

parapet

stucco

four-over-four double-hung sash

stepped windows · scroll-sawn bracket · vertical plank shutter · downspout · decorative cutout

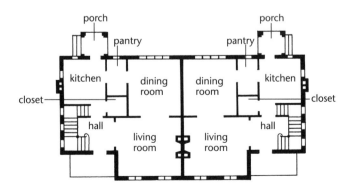

porch · porch

pantry · pantry

kitchen · dining room · dining room · kitchen

closet · closet

hall · living room · living room · hall

Anatomy of Fireproof Construction

terra-cotta
hollow tile

brick veneer

interior plaster

concrete
base

mortar line

concrete subfloor

concrete footing

In the early 1900s brick, cement, and asbestos shingles were marketed as economical "fireproof" choices for the small suburban house. To save money, brick and cement were often applied as a veneer (facing) on a groundwork of lath (wood or metal strips) over a standard wood balloon frame (see page 127). The balloon frame itself was not fireproof, however, and also tended to shift, causing the surface material to crack. One highly touted alternative was grooved terra-cotta (fired clay) tile block, which provided a firm base onto which brick veneer or cement could be directly applied—eliminating both wood frame and lath.

FIREPROOF HOUSE

diamond-pattern
asbestos shingles

hipped roof

dormer

projecting eaves

one-over-one
double-hung sash

hipped-roof
porch

pier

coping

cast
(molded)
cement

plate
glass

Bungalows and Small Houses

INGLENOOK

built-in bench

shelf molding

paneled door

random-width plank floor

grass-cloth panel

ceramic tile

DINING ROOM

decorative cutout

scalloped cornice board

exposed beams

dentil course

hand plate

random-width plank floor

built-in shelf

built-in cupboard

recessed swing door

OAK DOORS (INTERIOR)

colored glass

top rail

lead divider

lock plate

hanging stile

shutting stile

bottom rail

top rail

hanging stile

shutting stile

lock plate

inset panel

bottom rail

top rail

light

shutting stile

hanging stile

lock plate

top rail

shutting stile

hanging stile

lock plate

inset panel

bottom rail

Chapter Ten
Early Modernism

The period between World War I and World War II was one of strong contrasts. With the acceleration of industrialized technology came the wide availability of new materials such as plywood, reinforced concrete, steel, and chrome; mechanized building processes; and the prefabrication of standardized, interchangeable building elements. For the most part, however, the architectural taste of the mainstream remained stubbornly grounded in the predictable period revivals, which offered a comforting nostalgia in the face of the machine age. Modern European-based influences, such as Art Deco, only had a limited impact on single-family house design.

In the 1920s the modern movement began to gain momentum in the United States with the arrival of the Austrian architects Rudolph Schindler (1887–1953) and Richard Neutra (1892–1970) and the Swiss William Lescaze (1896–1969). They were joined in the 1930s by several Bauhaus architects, such as Ludwig Mies van der Rohe (1886–1969) and Walter Gropius (1883–1969), who were driven out of Europe by the Nazis. The work of these innovators represented the early tenets of the International Style, rooted in the cubic architecture of the Dutch De Stijl movement and the idealized industrial aesthetic of the Bauhaus, the German school of architecture Gropius had founded in 1919.

The International Style fully embraced the industrial ideal, advocating a clean break with the past. Progressive thinking, however, was slow to find a footing in America, and the geometrically precise aesthetic of early Modernism never had the same widespread acceptance for residential architecture as the familiar bungalows and cozy Dutch, Tudor, and Colonial houses of suburbia.

Early Modernism

CIRCULAR HOUSE

concrete

plasterboard

steel frame

plate glass

flagstone terrace

garage/workshop

bedroom

bedroom

den

closet

kitchen

bath

dining/living room

terrace

The precise mathematics and streamlined forms of geometry fascinated early Modernists, who experimented with new materials such as steel and plasterboard while trying to rework traditional floor plans to fit nontraditional shapes. The circular house shown here is based on a conceptual design submitted in a 1935 magazine contest. Instead of the more conventional concentration on the interior and its furnishings, the architect sought a "scientific solution" that related to the outdoors through ample use of glass. Topped by a dome, the garage was also round.

International Style

SUBURBAN HOUSE

flat tar-and-gravel roof   plate glass   glass block   steel sash   horizontal chimney

steel pipe railing

poured reinforced concrete

attached garage

planter box

stepped window

In 1932 Alfred Barr, Jr., the director of the Museum of Modern Art in New York, mounted a groundbreaking show called "Modern Architecture: International Exhibition," organized by the American architect Philip Johnson (b. 1906) and architectural historian Henry-Russell Hitchcock (1903–87). That exhibition gave the Modernist movement in Europe and the United States its name.

The phrase "less is more" is often invoked to explain the International style, which rejected all historical stylistic references in favor of clean, volumetric forms completely devoid of applied pattern, texture, and "superfluous" ornament. This mode of building, in which each element was defined as clearly as possible, was dependent on industrial technology. The use of steel and concrete as structural elements made the load-bearing wall unnecessary and encouraged the use of large expanses of glass. Filled with light, interiors were opened up and fitted with simple, often built-in furniture to keep the space flowing and free of clutter.

DINING AREA

curtain runner

steel sash

built-in shelf

platform

KITCHEN

glass block

stainless steel cupboard

stainless steel backsplash

stainless steel counter

checkerboard linoleum

Moderne

steel pipe railing

flat roof

asphalt banding

recessed entry

curved wall

glass door | plate glass | steel sash | downspout | steel casement

curved facade

closet

kitchen

bath

closet

hall

bedroom

living/dining room

porch

Making a short appearance in America in the 1930s, the smooth-surfaced, flat-roofed Moderne-style house was an essay in streamlined geometry, stripped of ornament except for an occasional frieze of horizontal grooves designed as "speed lines." Such streamlining was also reflected in curving wall planes. It expressed not only economy of line, but also a fascination with the aerodynamic speed and romance of the locomotive, the airplane, and the ocean liner (whose portholes often showed up as windows). In domestic architecture, the Moderne style was used primarily for small, single-family houses. These were found in the residential areas of small cities, in suburbs, and in seaside communities.

Moderne

SEASIDE HOUSE

steel railing

sunshade

one-over-one
double-hung sash

soffit

cantilevered
corner

portholes

clapboards

recessed entry porch

brick chimney

jalousie window
(adjustable glass louvers)

Art Deco

DOORS

lock plate

aluminum grille

kick plate

top rail

screen

push bar

hanging stile

shutting stile

bottom rail

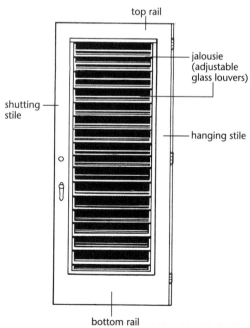

top rail

jalousie (adjustable glass louvers)

shutting stile

hanging stile

bottom rail

The term "Art Deco" derives from the title of a 1925 Paris design fair, called the *Exposition Internationale des Arts Décoratifs et Industriels Modernes* (*Arts Deco*, for short), where numerous rooms in the style were on display. Art Deco had begun to appear in Europe before World War I. It was a curious blend of Modernism, history, and fantasy, influenced by the speed-infused aesthetic of the Italian Futurists and the mystical images of Mayan, Assyrian, and Moorish cultures. These, in turn, were expressed by the richest of materials: marble, colored terrazzo, chrome, and ebony.

Adopted in America primarily in the 1930s, the Art Deco style was seldom used for single-family houses, but reached its apogee in New York, Los Angeles, and Miami, primarily in apartment buildings and city skyscrapers, which seemed best suited to this style of applied, concentrated decoration. Doorways, in particular, showed off the stylized forms and tropical motifs.

A-Frame

steep pitched roof

plate-glass gable

soffit

low-hanging eaves

rubblework masonry

wood shingles

extended beams

hopper windows (pivot in)

terrace

garage

hall

bath

kitchen

dining room

great room

terrace

In 1934 the architect Rudolph Schindler designed a modern weekend house for a client, Gisela Bennati, in Lake Arrowhead, California. A planned community, Lake Arrowhead required all new houses to be designed in the Norman Revival style (see page 193). Schindler responded rather sarcastically with a design dominated by a "Norman" roof that fell from the ridge all the way to the ground. Challenged by a dubious jury, the architect countered with photographs of steep-roofed houses, and as none of the panelists had ever been to France, he handily won the argument.

The result was the first A-frame built in America. True to the Modernist credo, Schindler sheathed the interior in one of the latest industrial products—plywood—and opened up the gable ends with large panes of glass. The open plan incorporated one large living/dining area and a built-in garage.

Chapter Eleven
The Postwar Era

The decades immediately following World War II constituted a boom era of unparalleled prosperity. This was, indeed, the dawn of the "affluent society," and no one was quicker to capitalize on it than the leaders of the housing industry. "DREAMS CAN COME TRUE!" promised the banner headline of the 1945 issue of the *Small Homes Annual*. The editors went on to assure their readers that the new stock plans offered on their pages were not for the cold, boxlike houses of the "modernistic" era. "They will be functional," they said, "but the primary function of a house is to be a *home*."

The house designs of the postwar era placed a new emphasis on comfort, efficiency, and informal "one-story living." The single-story house permitted shorter plumbing lines and heating ducts, eliminated annoying and hazardous stairs, and, most significant, allowed easy access to the yard or garden and the all-important patio barbecue.

As labor, land, and material prices climbed in the 1950s and 1960s, the search for more space at less cost eliminated halls and yielded the multi-use living/dining room, family room/kitchen, and guest room/study, as well as built-in storage units and furniture, the freestanding fireplace, the "conversation pit," and the carport. Experiments in open planning coincided with new developments in mass-produced materials, including reinforced concrete, long-span steel beams, particleboard, laminated wood, and plywood. The idea that technology and advanced engineering could solve any problem was wholeheartedly embraced, producing experiments in virtually every kind of construction.

Prefab Housing

TWO-FAMILY HOUSE

flat roof · projecting facade · one-over-one double-hung sash · galvanized steel sheeting · rib · brick veneer foundation · trellis · wood stoop · paneled steel door

After World War II, a severe housing shortage in America resulted in a market for pre-fabricated industrial homes that could be arranged in temporary settlements just outside existing developments. Not only were these cheap, but they could also be put up miraculously fast. The parts for the steel-sheathed "Palace" on this page, for example, were transported by truck from factory to building site. Within three hours of delivery, claimed the advertisement, the house, complete with furniture, conventional plumbing, heating, wiring, and kitchen appliances, was ready for two families. The prefab Quonset hut (see page 232) had few amenities and only a chemical toilet, but manufacturers claimed it was immune to sagging, warping, rotting, fire, and termites.

Prefab Housing

QUONSET HUT

asphalt-coated particleboard

louvered vent

ventilated air space

wood rafters (2x4)

domed roof

sunshade

lip

porch

asphalt-coated particle-
board over self-supporting
laminated wood arch

hopper window
(pivots in)

steel sash

concrete porch floor

closet

bath-
room

kitchen

bedroom

porch

closet

bed/
dressing
room

dining/living room

bedroom

pleated door

folding bed

DYMAXION DEPLOYMENT UNIT

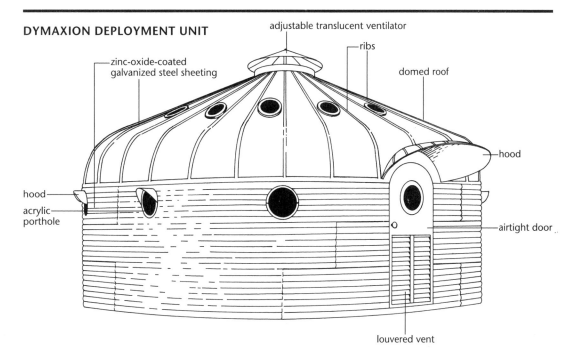

- adjustable translucent ventilator
- ribs
- zinc-oxide-coated galvanized steel sheeting
- domed roof
- hood
- hood
- acrylic porthole
- airtight door
- louvered vent

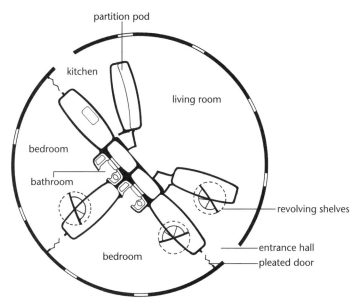

- partition pod
- kitchen
- living room
- bedroom
- bathroom
- revolving shelves
- entrance hall
- pleated door
- bedroom

In 1941 architect R. Buckminster Fuller (1895–1983) offered a new, improved version of a model house he had designed in 1927. Fuller claimed that the Dymaxion (from "dynamism," "maximum," and "ions") Deployment Unit II could house a small family at a cost of less than a dollar per square foot. The prefab Dymaxion house was built in reverse of the usual practice of ground up. First, the metal dome was assembled on the ground and raised on a temporary pole; the wall sections were then applied from the top down. The corrugated, galvanized steel shell was laminated inside with fiberglass insulation and the round portholes filled with plastic—the first time this high-priority World War II material was used anywhere other than in an airplane. The Dymaxion came complete with all the materials and a tool kit.

Prefab Housing

MOBILE HOME

streamlined corner   stovepipe   airtight door   steel sash   awning window (pivots out)   plate-glass slider

corrugated steel sheeting   trailer hitch

bathroom

bathroom

bedroom

living room/kitchen

bedroom

The first mass-produced mobile home, credited to the Covered Wagon Company of Detroit, appeared in America around 1933. This novel trailer had an inauspicious start, originally used as cheap, temporary housing in empty lots that were once called the "tin-can camps of Depression and wartime migrants." Trailer parks were not taken seriously until World War II, when such encampments were used to house thousands of workers in and around war-production centers. The trailer park, where people would often live in their mobile homes for years on end, gained a better reputation in the 1950s, when increasing numbers of professionals and retirees settled into these semipermanent communities. One other reason for respect: models over twenty-five feet long now had bathrooms. By the end of the 1950s, fully furnished models, with at least three rooms and a bath, sold for between $3,500 and $13,000.

Anatomy of "Good Construction"

subflooring

studs

joists

plate

wood sheathing

large-head nails

finished floorboards

waterproof building paper

wind brace

felt

brick veneer

subflooring

beam

cross bridging

end joist

joists

tar and pitch on felt

post

ledge

concrete footing

drain tile

cement waterproofing

concrete floor
(basement
level)

cement block

Immediately following World War II, there was increasing emphasis on the importance of "sound" building for small homes. This cutaway view, adapted from a 1945 building journal, was designed to educate the consumer on the underpinnings of a solidly built house. Although not visible, these "hidden values of good construction," advised the journal, should be demanded of all builders.

Ranch House

The ranch house was perhaps the ultimate symbol of the postwar American dream: a safe, affordable home promising efficiency and casual living. California architects introduced the "close-to-the-ground" ranch in the 1930s, evidently finding inspiration in the one-story plan of the Spanish rancho of the Southwest. By the late 1940s, this new house type had caught on across the country and still remains popular.

With its open kitchen/living area, the ranch was specifically geared to casual entertaining. Another key selling point was the desirable indoor/outdoor living promised by the one-story layout, which featured sliding glass doors, picture windows, and terraces and patios secluded in a rear yard. "The ability to move in and out of your house freely, without the hindrance of steps," boasted *Sunset* magazine's 1946 edition of *Western Ranch Houses*, "is one of the things that makes living in it pleasant and informal."

gles   pitched roof   concrete chimney   vertical siding

pane dow   paneled door   recessed entry porch   brick veneer   clapboards

BARBECUE PATIO

brick masonry   canvas awning panels   shed roof

barbecue

rubblework wall

firewood storage   grill   concrete floor

Ranch House

LIVING ROOM/KITCHEN

particleboard panels

exposed rafters

skylight

rubblework masonry

raised brick hearth

plate-glass sliders

fireplace

plank flooring

FIREPLACES

plaster over metal lath

galvanized steel hood

woven metal curtain

raised brick hearth

cast-iron grate

plaster over metal lath

damper control

raised flagstone hearth

steel corner plate

woven metal curtain

firebox

The Economical Small House

SMALL SUBURBAN HOUSE

shed roof

overhang

horizontal chimney

poured reinforced concrete

concrete shade arbor

plate glass

plate-glass slider

steel pole

hopper window (pivots in)

flagstone terrace

closet

kitchen

bath

bedroom

living room

garage

dining room

study

bedroom

terrace

bath

closet

closet

bedroom

terrace

Frequently built from mail-order plans, the economical small house of the postwar era offered a cheap alternative to the ranch house. Prospective buyers could leaf through plan books and magazines; choose a model named the "Monarch," the "Tarry," or perhaps the "Alpine;" and for the price of a stamp and a few dollars become the proud owners of a complete set of working blueprints and specifications.

Houses built from stock plans were touted as "pretested," offering a fine "custom" design without the considerable cost of hiring a professional architect. To keep prices down, the plan companies specified inexpensive factory-made plywood or prefab wood siding and stucco. The convenient one-story plan proliferated, but there was also the new split-level, or "hi-ranch design" (see page 242). This boasted vinyl tile floors, interior walls of gypsum (plasterboard), and a lower level often designed to be left unfinished until the space was needed.

The Economical Small House

SMALL SUBURBAN HOUSE

fixed multipane picture window

asphalt shingles

horizontal chimney

hipped roof

pivoting windows

gutter

brick veneer

recessed entry porch

trellis

hollow-core door

downspout

Anatomy of Brick Veneer

A veneer, or facing layer, of masonry is an economical alternative to a solid three-dimensional bond (see page 69) because it requires much less material. Here, the brick veneer is applied over a wood frame, which provides the support for the building. The veneer is one layer of bricks thick.

wood studs

weatherboard

waterproof building paper

sole plate

subflooring

joist

end joist

sill

brick veneer

concrete foundation

ledge

The Economical Small House

SMALL SUBURBAN HOUSE

louvered vent

jalousie window
(adjustable
glass louvers)

low-pitched
tar-and-
gravel roof

boxed eaves

awning window
(pivots out)

carport

brick built-in planter wall

rough stucco

storage

carport

kitchen

terrace

living room

bedroom

bath

closet

bedroom

The Economical Small House

SPLIT-LEVEL HOUSE

pitched roof

six-over-six double hung sash

paneled shutter

transom

shed roof

squared oriel

wood shingles

plate-glass picture window

overhang

vertical plank siding

paneled garage door

stoop

MAIN FLOOR

patio

bath

bedroom

bath-room

kitchen

bedroom

bedroom

living/ dining room

REGENCY-STYLE HOUSE

multipane transom

hipped roof

brick chimney

twelve-over-twelve
double-hung sash

flat roof

white-
washed
brick

French door
(full-length casement)

louvered shutter

paneled door

Although new ideas meant new designs in the postwar era, traditional styles never lost their popularity. The low-slung Regency-style house, above, with its floor-to-ceiling windows, was especially well suited to comfortable one-story living. As always, Colonial-style houses were in demand, especially reproductions of houses from Williamsburg, the restored capital of 18th-century Virginia that had been opened as the country's first outdoor museum in 1926.

All designs, of course, were freely updated for "modern" living. "If cooking's going to be fun," wrote one designer of a small traditional house in 1954, "we might as well make a family room out of the kitchen."

The Traditional House

WILLIAMSBURG-STYLE HOUSE

chimney cap

brick chimney

pitched-roof dormer

steep pitched roof

split wood shingles

pediment

boxed eaves

modillion course

clapboards

colonette   entry porch   Chinese Chippendale railing

brick foundation

nine-over-nine double-hung sash

LIVING ROOM

scalloped valance   cornice molding   patterned wallpaper

bay window

mantel

wainscot

tile facing

inset panel   corner cupboard

brick firebox

The Traditional House

COLONIAL-STYLE HOUSE

six-over-six double-hung sash

pitched roof

triangular window

split wood shingles

trellis

recessed porch

louvered shutter

paneled door

clapboards

KITCHEN

scalloped cornice board

stainless steel cabinet

light fixture

plastic laminate countertop

range hood

backsplash

checkerboard vinyl floor

Anatomy of a Platform Frame

common rafters

load-bearing wall

studs

sole plate

subflooring

double top plate

cripple stud

header

trimmer stud

rough window opening

sill

plywood wall sheathing

plywood subflooring

cripple stud

concrete block foundation wall

joists

concrete footing

end joist

sole plate

corner studs

Emerging in the postwar era and still in use, the platform frame differs from the balloon frame (see page 127) primarily in that the vertical studs are only one story high. The floors are built as separate units, or platforms, and the one-story studs, of 2 x 4–inch lumber, run between a bottom sole plate and a double top plate. Often, a wall of plates and studs is assembled horizontally, then raised into place as a complete unit. This makes a more rigid system than the balloon frame and is simpler to build.

Anatomy of a Truss

truss clip

rafter

king post

strut

side post

bottom chord

KING POST TRUSS

struts

truss clip

rafter

bottom chord

"W" TRUSS

king post

strut

truss clip

side post

rafter

SCISSORS TRUSS

Use of the prefabricated roof truss has increased since the 1950s as an alternative to individual rafters, which require more skill, time, and lumber. Spaced the length of the roof at about two-foot intervals, most trusses are composed of triangles, shapes that will not distort under heavy loads. The three variations above commonly used for pitched roofs, look similar, but the web pattern in each actually distributes force quite differently; thus, each is rated for different loads and spans.

The Futuristic Home

GEODESIC DOME

acrylic skylight

domed roof

coated plywood panels

acrylic transom

acrylic porthole

vertical plank siding

shed-sided entry porch

While tradition held through the 1950s and 1960s, innovative designers were always looking for new expressions. As the space age unfolded, visions of the ultra-modern future captured the American imagination, sometimes inspiring house designs that would have looked more at home on other planets than on Earth. New building methods made virtually any structural feat possible, and bizarre shapes were no problem. Most fell by the wayside, but the geodesic dome (above), patented by Buckminster Fuller in 1954, caught on in the 1960s, and by the next decade more than 80,000 sets of plans for dome homes had been sold.

bedroom

bedroom

living room

hall

bathroom

dining room/ kitchen

entry porch

The Futuristic Home

BUBBLE HOUSE

stovepipe

plate-glass window

sprayed concrete (over balloon form)

hopper window (pivots in)

The bubble house was based on a construction technique known as Airform, patented by California architect Wallace Neff around 1940 and used sporadically in the 1950s. After the foundation was poured, a balloon was stretched over a steel cable, inflated, coated with reinforcing, then sprayed with concrete. A compressor kept the balloon full until the concrete had set, and then the balloon was deflated and removed.

bed-room

bath-room

alcove

bath-room

bed-room

partition

kitchen

living/dining room

The Futuristic Home

EARTH-SHELTERED HOUSE

flat precast concrete roof (earth covered)

passive solar collector panel

turbine ventilator

plate-glass picture window

bathroom

laundry

bathroom

kitchen

storage

closet

entrance tunnel

bedroom

bedroom

bedroom

living/dining room

closet

concrete-pipe retaining walls

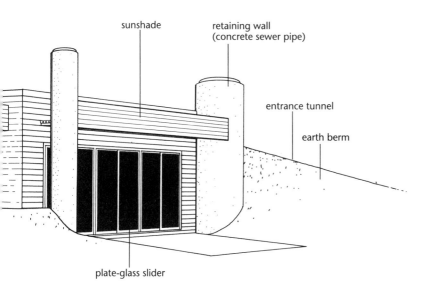

sunshade

retaining wall
(concrete sewer pipe)

entrance tunnel

earth berm

plate-glass slider

**CONSTRUCTION
DETAIL**

(FRONT)

metal flashing

plywood curb

fiberglass insulation

steel truss

sun-
shade

roll-up
sunshade

waterproofing

heat duct

concrete-pipe retaining wall

earth

drainage layer (sand or gravel)

plywood support fin

rigid insulation

concrete plank

concrete block

(BACK)

The concept of the quiet, energy-efficient, earth-sheltered house, in which the roof and at least three sides of the structure are covered with soil, was developed in the early 1960s as an outgrowth of atomic fallout shelters, and its popularity grew in the next decades with increased awareness of environmental concerns. The primary building material is typically concrete, which acts as a thermal mass. The insulating soil helps warm the structure in cool weather and draws heat out in warm months. Solar panels collect and store natural energy, while south-facing windows capture low-angle winter sunlight.

Chapter Twelve
Contemporary Trends

America's era of post–World War II affluence had come to a definite end by the 1970s. One major reason was the Vietnam War; as military activity increased overseas and energy costs skyrocketed at home, the United States went into a deep economic recession. Many small architectural firms closed, and those that survived increasingly sought economical alternative designs, developing solar technology in tandem with the growing interest in environmentalism, and turning to adaptive redesign of old buildings for new uses.

At an individual level, architects in the 1960s and 1970s were still exploring Modernist expressions. Dissatisfaction was growing, however, as it became increasingly apparent that an abstract approach often failed to take into account the needs and effects of specific sites, climates, and materials. In 1975 an exhibition of project drawings from the Ecole des Beaux-Arts mounted by the Museum of Modern Art in New York recognized and confirmed the interest in a return to architectural ornament and traditional academic solutions to building problems.

This trend had already become evident in Postmodern architecture, which emerged in the 1960s in reaction to the stark aesthetic of the International style. Mies van der Rohe reportedly had declared "Less is more" in the 1920s, but forty years later the Philadelphia architect Robert Venturi (b. 1925) countered with "Less is a bore." To the Postmodernist eyes of Venturi and many others, ornament and historical references set a mood, providing wit and a sense of scale and interest, and also humanized a building. Neither movement is dead. The tension between respect for the lessons of history and the quest for originality and modern, independent expression continues today.

SEASIDE HOUSE

cylindrical stairwell

skylight

flat roof

plate glass

recessed window

cedar siding

plate-glass slider

pipe railing

cantilevered balcony

enclosed stair

cylindrical deck

Most moderately priced housing built in the 1960s and 1970s was limited to the popular one-story and traditional styles of the postwar era. Among higher-end clients, however, architectural firms found an interest in sophisticated modern designs that continued to reinvent abstract, cubic architecture. In fresh interpretations, architects began to break the box with sculptural forms that had an almost machinelike clarity. Technology allowed increasing experimentation with shapes, scale, dimensions, and complex multi-level plans.

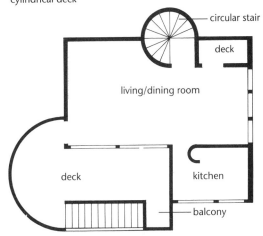

circular stair

deck

living/dining room

deck

kitchen

balcony

Modernism

SEASIDE HOUSE

paired chimney cylinders

roof terrace

sunshade

recessed entry

plate glass

Modernism

flat roof

concrete block

FIRST FLOOR

entry

garage

kitchen

garage

family room

raised sitting area

living/dining room

fireplace

entry

SECOND FLOOR

bath-room

bed-room

bath

bath

bed-room

bed-room

hall

bath

bed-room

roof terrace

upper living room

bed-room

Modernism

SOLAR HOUSE

passive solar collector panel

plate-glass gable

exposed rafters

plate glass

clapboards

deck

deck

screened porch

stilt

concrete foundation

bedroom

bath

kitchen

laundry

deck

closets

vestibule

bedroom

living/family room

deck

screened porch

deck

Modernism

SOLAR HOUSE

- passive solar collector panel
- pitched roof
- brick chimney
- clerestory window
- cedar siding
- balcony
- asphalt shingles
- sliding sash
- plate-glass slider
- deck
- concrete foundation

- closet
- bath
- entry
- kitchen
- bedroom
- dining room
- living room
- deck
- deck

Modernism

brick chimney

broken gable

clerestory window

plate glass

shed roof

plate-glass slider

diagonal clapboards

Anatomy of Asphalt-Shingled Roofing

Because it is inexpensive and waterproof, asphalt is a commonly used roofing material. As opposed to individual wood shingles, or shakes, asphalt shingles are typically made as butt strips with three tabs at the lower edge. When overlapped, the tabs appear as individual shingles.

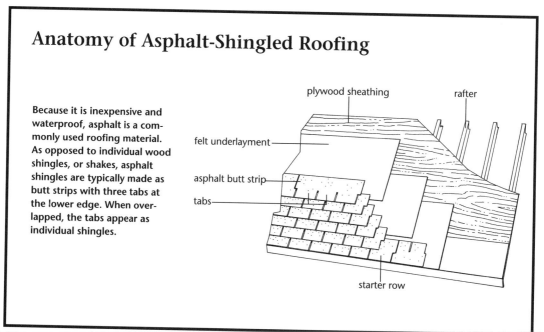

plywood sheathing

rafter

felt underlayment

asphalt butt strip

tabs

starter row

SEASIDE HOUSE

steep pitched roof

clerestory window

soffit

fascia board

projecting eaves

half-round window

mullion

plate glass

weathered wood shingles

six-over-six double-hung sash

Postmodernism is a contextual architecture in which a house design is developed with specific regard to the site, the design of neighboring structures, and climatic conditions. Designs often draw on local building types, such as the Florida Cracker House (see pages 112–113) as well as colonial architectural and American vernacular modes such as the Shingle and Stick styles. This interest coincided with a growing preservation movement in America, which gained momentum with the National Historic Preservation Act of 1966.

In contrast to previous revival movements, Postmodernism has a sense of humor and an attitude —a certain chip on its shoulder that gives the style its edge. Turned out in Pompeiian colors, designs might make liberal use of such traditional Classical vocabulary as the pediment and the Palladian window, but the familiar forms are deliberately exaggerated, overblown, flattened, or designed to look broken or eroded. This is a style of applied ornament in which decoration does not require a specific purpose. Designers have been criticized for rummaging among various styles and combining elements in an indiscriminate and superficial pastiche. At its best, however, Postmodernism is stark and original and represents a return to "humanized" design.

The movement reached its height of popularity in the 1970s and 1980s. Its playful qualities made it particularly well suited to beach houses.

Postmodernism

pipe chimney

hipped roof

asphalt shingles

clerestory window

acroterion

soffit

projecting eaves

stucco over concrete block

plate glass

plywood board-and-batten siding

industrial steel sash

glass-block pocket

multipane door

FIRST FLOOR

bath-room

laundry

bedroom

bedroom

SECOND FLOOR

kitchen

living/dining room

SEASIDE HOUSE

pitched roof

cupola

stickwork

hipped roof (ribbed tin)

projecting eaves

exposed rafter tails

fascia board

two-over-two
double-hung sash

pediment

clapboards

pilaster

plate glass

screened
porch

globe finial

stickwork

porch

bath

living/
dining
room

kitchen

screened
porch

Postmodernism

LOFT BEDROOM

pass-through shelf

platform bed

picture molding

drop hatch

metal pipe

baseboard

tread — riser

LIVING ROOM

pass-through shelf

painted cardboard capital

plate glass

"eroded" plasterboard wall

planter box

painted cardboard sonetube (poured concrete mold)

FIREPLACES

quarter-round log
(thin plywood bend over braces)

faux wood
paint finish

soldier bricks

slate hearth   firebox

painted
plasterboard

painted
plywood
mantel

faux marble
paint finish

wood ball

firebox   paper fan   hearth

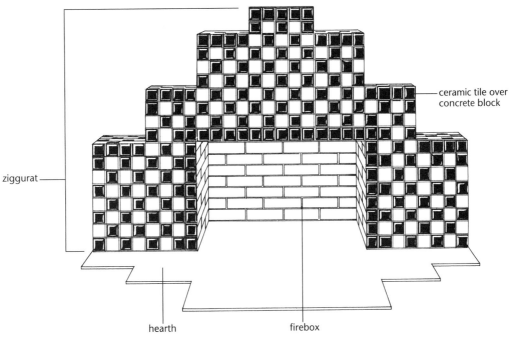

ceramic tile over
concrete block

ziggurat

hearth   firebox

Bibliography

BOOKS

Ahrens, Donna; Tom Ellison; and Ray Sterling. *Earth-Sheltered Homes*. New York: Van Nostrand Reinhold, 1981.

Andrews, Ralph. *Curtis' Western Indians*. New York: Bonanza Books, 1952.

Andrews, Wayne. *Architecture, Ambition, and Americans*. New York: Free Press, 1978.

The Architectural Treasures of Early America. Harrisburg, Pa.: National Historical Society, 1987.

Barber, George Franklin. *George F. Barber's Cottage Souvenir Number Two*. Watkins Glen, N.Y.: American Life, 1982.

Barns, Cass. *The Sod House*. Lincoln: University of Nebraska Press, 1930.

Bealer, Alex. *The Log Cabin: Homes of the American Wilderness*. Barre, Mass.: Barre Publications, 1978.

Benjamin, Asher. *The American Builder's Companion*. New York: Dover Publications, 1969. Reprint of 6th edition (R. P. & C. Williams, 1827).

———. *The Architect, or Practical House Carpenter (1830)*. New York: Dover Publications, 1988. Reprint of 1830 edition.

The Book of a Hundred Houses. New York: Duffield, 1906.

The Book of Little Houses. New York: MacMillan, 1915.

Brown, Henry Collins. *Book of Home-Building and Decoration*. Garden City, N.Y.: Doubleday, Page, 1912.

Bunting, Bainbridge. *Early Architecture of New Mexico*. Albuquerque: University of New Mexico Press, 1976.

———. *Taos Adobes*. Albuquerque: University of New Mexico Press, 1992.

Caemmerer, Alex. *The Houses of Key West*. Sarasota, Fla.: Pineapple Press, 1992.

Comstock, William T. *Victorian Domestic Architectural Plans and Details*. New York: Dover Publications, 1987. Reprint of *Modern Architectural Designs and Details* (New York: Architectural Publisher, 1881).

Cummings, Abbott Lowell. *The Framed Houses of Massachusetts Bay, 1625–1725*. Cambridge, Mass., and London: Belknap Press of Harvard University Press, 1979.

Davidson, Marshall. *The American Heritage History of Notable American Houses*. New York: American Heritage Publishing, 1971.

Dickinson, Duo. *The Small House*. New York: McGraw-Hill, 1986.

Downing, A. J. *The Architecture of Country Houses*. New York: Da Capo Press, 1969. Reprint of 1850 edition (New York: D. Appleton).

Downing, Antoinette, and Vincent Scully, Jr. *The Architectural Heritage of Newport, Rhode Island*. New York: American Legacy Press, 1982.

Driver, Harold. *Indians of North America*. Chicago: University of Chicago Press, 1925.

Ehrsam, Fritz. *The Swiss Chalet in America*. Reading, Pa., 1916.

Fink, Augusta. *Adobes in the Sun*. San Francisco: Chronicle Books, 1972.

500 Small Houses of the Twenties. New York: Dover Publications, 1990. Reprint of *The Books of a Thousand Homes*, vol. 1. New York: Home Owners Service Institute, 1923.

Fleming, John; Hugh Honor; and Nicholaus Pevsner. *A Dictionary of Architecture*. Middlesex, England: Penguin Books, 1966.

Foley, Mary Mix. *The American House*. New York: Harper & Row, 1980.

Ford, James, and Katherine Ford. *The Modern House in America*. New York: Architectural Book Publishing, 1940.

Forman, Henry. *Early Manor and Plantation Houses of Maryland*. Eastern Maryland: Private printing, n.d.

Fowler, Orson S. *The Octagon House*. New York: Dover Publications, 1973. Reprint of *A Home for All* (1853).

Gamble, Robert. *The Alabama Catalogue: Historic American Buildings Survey*. Tuscaloosa: University of Alabama Press, 1987.

Gillon, Edmund V., Jr. *Pictorial Archive of Early Illustrations and Views of American Architecture*. New York: Dover Publications, 1971.

Glassie, Henry. *Pattern in the Material Folk Culture of the Eastern United States*. Philadelphia: University of Pennsylvania Press, 1968.

Gordon-Van Tine Co. *117 House Designs of the Twenties*. New York: Dover Publications, 1992. Reprint of *Gordon-Van Tine Homes* (Davenport, Iowa: Gordon-Van Tine Co., 1923).

Great Georgian Houses of America, vols. 1–2. New York: Kalkhoff Press, 1933, 1937.

Greene and Greene. *The Architecture and Related Designs of Charles Sumner Greene and Henry Mather Greene: 1894–1934*. Los Angeles: Los Angeles Municipal Art Gallery, 1977.

Grow, Lawrence. *Classic Old House Plans*. Pittstown, N.J.: Main Street Press, 1978, 1984.

——— and Dina Von Zweck. *American Victorian*. New York: Harper & Row, 1984.

Haase, Ronald. *Classic Cracker*. Sarasota, Fla.: Pineapple Press, 1992.

Hamlin, Talbot. *Greek Revival Architecture in America*. New York: Oxford University Press, 1944.

Handlin, David. *The American Home*. Boston: Little, Brown, 1979.

Hannaford, Donald, and Revel Edwards. *Spanish Colonial or Adobe Architecture of California 1800–1850*. New York: Architectural Book Publishing, 1931.

Harris, Cyril. M.,ed. *Illustrated Dictionary of Historic Architecture*. New York: Dover Publications, 1977.

Hatton, Hap. *Tropical Splendor*. New York: Knopf, 1987.

Historic American Buildings Survey in Indiana. Bloomington: Indiana University Press, 1983.

Historic American Buildings Survey: New York. New York: Garland Publications, 1979.

Historic American Buildings Survey: Northern Illinois, 1833–1872. Washington, D.C.: National Park Service, 1936–37.

Historic American Buildings Survey: Texas Catalogue. San Antonio: Trinity University Press, 1974.

Hitchcock, Henry-Russell. *Architecture: Nineteenth and Twentieth Centuries*. Middlesex, England: Penguin Books, 1958.

Hofsinde, Robert. *Indians at Home*. New York: William Morrow, 1964.

House and Garden's Book of Houses. New York: Condé Nast, 1920.

Hubka, Thomas. *Big House, Little House, Back House, Barn*. Hanover, N.H.: University Press of New England, 1984.

Jensen, Robert. *Ornamentalism: The New Decorativeness in Architecture and Design*. New York: Clarkson Potter, 1982.

Jordy, William. *American Buildings and Their Architects: Progressive and Academic Ideals at the Turn of the Twentieth Century*. Garden City, N.Y.: Anchor Books, 1976.

Kauffman, Henry. *Architecture of the Pennsylvania Dutch Country 1700–1900*. Elverson, Pa.: Old Springfield Shoppe, 1992.

Keefe, Charles, ed. *The American House*. New York: U.P.C. Book Company, 1922.

Kelly, J. Frederick. *Early Domestic Architecture of Connecticut*. New York: Dover Publications, 1963.

Lafever, Minard. *The Beauties of Modern Architecture*. New York: Da Capo Press, 1968. Reprint of 3rd edition (New York: D. Appleton, 1839).

Lancaster, Clay. *The American Bungalow*. New York: Abbeville Press, 1985.

———. *Antebellum Architecture of Kentucky*. Lexington: University Press of Kentucky, 1991.

Lavine, Sigmund. *The Houses the Indians Built*. New York: Dodd, Mead, 1975.

Lewis, Arnold. *American Country Houses of the Gilded Age*. New York: Dover Publications, 1982. Reprint of George William Sheldon's *Artistic Country-Seats* (New York: D. Appleton, 1886–87).

Lockwood, Charles. *Bricks and Brownstone: The New York Row House, 1783–1929*. New York: McGraw-Hill, 1972.

Makinson, Randell. *Greene and Greene*. Salt Lake City: Peregrine Smith, 1979.

Manucy, Albert. *The Houses of St. Augustine*. Gainsville: University Press of Florida, 1978. Reprint of 1962 edition, sponsored by St. Augustine Historical Society.

Mayhew, Edgar, and Minor Meyers, Jr. *A Documentary History of American Interiors from the Colonial Era to 1915*. New York: Charles Scribner's Sons, 1980.

McCalester, Virginia, and Lee McCalester. *A Field Guide to American Houses*. New York: Alfred A. Knopf, 1984.

McCoy, Esther. *Five California Architects*. New York: Reinhold Publishing, 1961.

McDermott, John, ed. *The French in the Mississippi Valley*. Champaign: University of Illinois Press, 1965.

McKee, Harley. *Introduction to Early American Masonry*. Washington, D.C.: National Trust for Historic Preservation and Columbia University, 1973.

Metz, Don, ed. *The Compact House Book*. Pownal, Vt.: Garden Way Publishing, 1983.

Mohney, David, and Keller Esterling, eds. *Seaside: Making a Town in America*. New York: Princeton Architectural Press, 1991.

A Monograph of the Works of McKim, Mead & White, 1879–1915. New York: Da Capo Press, 1985. Reprint of 1925 edition (New York: Architectural Book Publishing).

Monteil, W. L. *Kentucky Folk Architecture*. Lexington: University Press of Kentucky, 1976.

Morgan, Lewis. *Houses and House-Life of the American Aborigines*. Chicago: University of Chicago Press, 1915.

Morrison, Hugh. *Early American Architecture from the First Colonial Settlements to the National Period*. New York: Oxford University Press, 1952.

Nabokov, Peter, and Robert Easton. *Native American Architecture*. New York: Oxford University Press, 1989.

The Natco Double House. Boston: Rogers & Manson, 1914.

New England Begins: The Seventeenth Century, vol. 2. Boston: Museum of Fine Arts, 1982.

New Orleans Architecture, vols. 4 and 6. Gretna, La.: Pelican Publishing, 1974.

New York City Landmarks Preservation Commission. *Guide to New York City Landmarks*. Washington, D.C.: Preservation Press, 1992.

Newcomb, Rexford. *Old Kentucky Architecture*. New York: W. Helburn, 1940.

Newport Mansions: The Gilded Age. Little Compton, R.I.: Foremost Publishers, 1982.

Nichols, Frederick. *The Architecture of Georgia*. Savannah: Beehive Press, 1976.

Noble, Allen. *Wood, Brick and Stone: The North American Settlement Landscape*, vol. 1: *Houses*. Amherst: University of Massachusetts Press, 1984.

Oringderff, Barbara. *True Sod: Sod Houses of Kansas*. North Neton, Kans.: Mennonite Press, 1976.

Patterson, Augusta Owen. *American Homes of Today*. New York: MacMillan, 1924.

Perrin, Richard. *The Architecture of Wisconsin*. Madison: State Historical Society of Wisconsin, 1967.

Pierson, William H., Jr. *American Buildings and Their Architects: The Colonial and Neo-Classical Styles*. Garden City, N.Y.: Anchor Books, 1976.

———. *American Buildings and Their Architects: Technology and the Picturesque; the Corporate and the Early Gothic Styles*. Garden City, N.Y. : Doubleday, 1978.

Pomada, Elizabeth, and Michael Larson. *Painted Ladies*. New York: E. P. Dutton, 1978.

Radford's Artistic Homes. Chicago: Radford Architectural Company, 1908.

Rawson, Richard. *The Old House Book of Barn Plans*. New York: Sterling Publishing, 1990.

Rifkind, Carole. *A Field Guide to American Architecture*. New York: New American Library, 1980.

Roth, Leland. *A Concise History of American Architecture*. New York: Harper & Row, 1979.

Schwartz, Marvin. *The Jan Martense Schenck House*. Brooklyn: Brooklyn Institute of Arts and Sciences, 1964.

Scully, Vincent, Jr. *American Architecture and Urbanism*. New York: Holt, Rinehart & Winston, 1969.

———. *The Shingle Style and the Stick Style*. New Haven: Yale University Press, 1955, 1971.

Seale, William. *Recreating the Historic House Interior*. Nashville: American Association for State and Local History, 1979.

Selected Houses from PA. New York: Reinhold Publishing, n.d.

Sexton, R. W. *Spanish Influence on American Architecture and Decoration*. New York: Brentano's, 1927.

Shephard, Augustus. *Camps in the Woods*. New York: Architectural Book Publishing, 1931.

Silver, Nathan. *Lost New York*. Boston: Houghton Mifflin, 1967.

Sloan, Samuel. *Sloan's Victorian Buildings*. New York: Dover Publications, 1980. Reprint of *The Model Architect* (Philadelphia: E. S. Jones, 1852).

Stotz, Charles. *The Early Architecture of Western Pennsylvania*. W. Helburn, 1936.

Stoudt, John. *Early Pennsylvania Arts and Crafts*. New York: A. S. Barnes, 1964.

Swank, Scott. *Arts of the Pennsylvania Germans*. New York: W. W. Norton, 1983.

Twenty-five Years of Record Houses. New York: McGraw-Hill, 1978.

Upton, Dell, ed. *America's Architectural Roots*. Washington, D.C.: Preservation Press, 1986.

——— and John Michael Vlach, eds. *Common Places: Readings in American Vernacular Architecture*. Athens, Ga.: University of Georgia Press, 1986.

Walker, Lester. *American Shelter*. Woodstock, N.Y.: Overlook Press, 1981.

Warren, Nancy Hunter. *New Mexico Style*. Santa Fe: Museum of New Mexico Press, 1986.

Wells, Sharon, and Lawson Little. *Portraits: Wooden Houses of Key West*. Key West: Historic Key West Preservation Board, 1979.

White, Jon. *Everyday Life of the North American Indians*. New York: Dorset Press, 1979.

Wicks, William. *Log Cabins: How to Build and Furnish Them*. New York: Forest & Stream Publishing, 1889.

Wills, Royal Barry. *Living on the Level: One-Story Houses*. Cambridge, Mass.: Houghton Mifflin, 1954.

———. *More Houses for Good Living*. New York: Architectural Book Publishing, 1968.

Wilson, Samuel, Jr. *The Architecture of Colonial Louisiana: Collected Essays*. Lafayette, La.: Center for Louisiana Studies, University of Southwestern Louisiana, 1987.

———. *Gulf Coast Architecture*. Department of State, Historic Pensacola Preservation Board.

Woodbridge, Sally. *California Architecture: Historic American Buildings Survey*. San Francisco: Chronicle Books, 1988.

Wright, Frank Lloyd. *Drawings and Plans of Frank Lloyd Wright*. New York: Dover Publications, 1983. Reprint of *Ausgefuhrte Bauten und Entwurfe von Frank Lloyd Wright* (Berlin: Ernst Wasmuth, 1910).

Wright, Richardson, ed. *House and Garden's Book of Houses*. New York: Condé Nast, 1915.

ARTICLES

Boyd, Elizabeth. "Fireplaces and Stoves in Colonial New Mexico." *El Palacio*, vol. 65, no. 6, 1958.

Bucher, Robert. "The Continental Log House." *Pennsylvania Folklife*, vol. 12, no. 4, Summer 1962.

———. "The Swiss Bank House in America." *Pennsylvania Folklife*, vol. 18, 1969.

Bushnell, David., Jr. "Native Villages and Village Sites East of the Mississippi." *Bureau of American Ethnology Bulletin*, no. 69. Washington, D.C.: Government Printing Office, Smithsonian Institute, 1919.

Gulliford, Andrew. "Sod Houses." *Fine Homebuilding*, Feb.–March 1986.

Landau, Sarah Bradford. "Richard Morris Hunt, the Continental Picturesque, and the 'Stick Style.'" *Journal of the Society of Architectural Historians*, Oct. 1983.

Long, Amos, Jr. "Bake-Ovens in the Pennsylvania Folk Culture." *Pennsylvania Folklife*, Dec. 1964.

Noble, Allen. "Pioneer Settlement on the Plains: Sod Dugouts and Sod Houses." *Pioneer America Society Transactions*, 1981.

Peterson, Charles. "Early St. Genevieve and Its Houses." *Missouri Historical Review*, vol. 35, Jan. 1941.

———. "French Houses of the Illinois Country." *Missouriana*, Aug.–Sept. 1938.

Weaver, William Woys. "The Pennsylvania German House." *Winterthur Portfolio*, vol. 21, no. 4, Winter 1986.

PERIODICALS

American Architect, vols. 1–3, 5, 7–8 (1919–27).

Amercian Architect and Building News, vols. 1–152 (1876–1938).

American Homes and Gardens, vols. 1–12, (1905–15).

The Architectural Forum (1935–38).

Architectural Record (1892–1945).

The Architectural Review and American Builder's Journal, vols. 1, 3 (1868–70).

The Craftsman (Feb. 1905).

The House Beautiful, vols. 16–81 (1904–76).

House and Garden, vols. 3–145 (1903–45).

Whitehead, Russell F., ed. *The White Pine Series of Architectural Monographs*, vols. 9 (no. 3)–17 (no. 6). St. Paul, Minn.: White Pine Bureau, 1921–31.

Credits

ABBREVIATIONS AND NOTATIONS
AIA (adapted from photos and measured drawings, The White Pine Monograph Series, Collected and Edited by Russell F. Whitehead, The George P. Lindsay Collection, The American Institute of Architects Library and Archives, Washington, D.C.); AMNH (adapted from photo, American Museum of Natural History); BL (adapted from photo, Bancroft Library, University of California, Berkeley); HABS (adapted from drawings, Historic American Buildings Survey); MAI (adapted from photo, Museum of the American Indian); NTHP (adapted from building, National Trust for Historic Preservation); SI (adapted from photo, Smithsonian Institute); SPNEA (adapted from building or object, Society for the Preservation of New England Antiquities); UA (adapted from photo, University of Arizona).

CHAPTER 1 15 Engraving, Village of Pomeiooc, 1590, Smithsonian Institute. 16 (top, center) MAI; (bottom) BL, in *Native American Architecture* by Peter Nabokov & Robert Easton (New York: Oxford University Press, 1989). 17 (top) adapted from *Houses and House-Life of the American Aborigines* by Lewis Morgan (Chicago: University of Chicago Press, 1915); (center) adapted from *Indians at Home* by Robert Hosfinde (New York: William Morrow, 1964); (bottom) adapted from photo (Edward S. Curtis) in *Curtis' Western Indians* by Ralph Andrews (New York: Bonanza Books, 1952). 20 (center left) adapted from *Indians of North America* by Harold Driver (Chicago: University of Chicago Press, 1961); (bottom) adapted from engraving "Cherokee Settlement of Toqua," SI, in *Native American Architecture*. 21 (top, bottom) MAI. 22 (top) adapted from *Houses and House-Life of the American Aborigines*; (bottom left) AMNH, in *Native American Architecture*; (bottom right) adapted from *Indians of North America*. 23 (top) MAI; (center left) adapted from *Everyday Life of the North American Indians* by Jon White (New York: Dorset Press, 1979); (center right) adapted from photo (S. McAlister) in *Native American Architecture*; (bottom) adapted from *The Houses the Indians Built* by Sigmund Lavine (New York: Dodd, Mead, 1975). 24 (top) UA, (center) AMNH, both in *Native American Architecture*; (bottom) adapted from *The Houses the Indians Built*.

CHAPTER 2 28 (bottom), 29 adapted from *The Houses of St. Augustine* by Albert Manucy (Gainsville: University Press of Florida, 1962). 30 (bottom) adapted from *Early Architecture of New Mexico* by Bainbridge Bunting (Albuquerque: University of New Mexico Press, 1976). 31 (top) interior, El Rancho de las Golondrinas, La Cienega, N.M. 32 adapted from photos in *New Mexico Style* by Nancy Hunter Warren (Santa Fe: Museum of New Mexico Press, 1986). 36 DeWint House, Rockland County, N.Y., 1700, HABS (Daniel Hopping). 37 (top) door, Bennett House, Brooklyn, 1766, HABS (Carl Stove); (bottom left) door, Jackson Jones Homestead, Wantaugh, N.Y., HABS (Charles Hoffman); (bottom right) door, DuMond House, Hurley, N.Y., HABS (A. Schrowang). 38 adapted from drawing (Ian Smith), based on Schenck House, Brooklyn, c. 1670, in *The Jan Martense Schenck House* by Marvin Schwartz (Brooklyn: Brooklyn Institute of Arts and Sciences, 1964). 39 (bottom right) plan, Nicolas Haring Barn, Rockleigh, N.J., HABS. 43 Schaeffer House, Schaefferstown, Pa., c. 1736. 44 section view based on research by Albert T. Gamon. 45 Fort Zeller, Wernersville, Pa., 1745. 46–47 Oley Forge Ironmaster's Mansion, Oley, Pa., adapted from measured drawings by

Kenneth LeVan. 48 Peter Wentz Farmstead, Worcester, Pa., 1758. 49 bakehouse, Christian Herr House, Lampeter Township, Pa. 50–51 (bottom) plan, David Stauffer Barn, Butler County, Pa., HABS. 52–53, 56, 57 (bottom) based on research by Charles E. Peterson. 55 (bottom) plan, Riverlake Plantation, Pointe Coupee Parish, La., c. 1820, HABS (Sid Gray). 57 (top) Roque House, Nachitoches, La., mid-1700s, adapted from photo (J. Alphonse Prudhomme) in *America's Architectural Roots*, ed. Dell Upton (Washington, D.C.: Preservation Press, 1986). 58, 60, 61 Oakland Plantation, Nachitoches, La., HABS (Cynthia Steward, Jeffrey Solak). 59 Saribault Cabin, Murphy's Landing State Park, Minn., adapted from photos (Jim Mone) in *The Log Cabin: Homes of the American Wilderness* by Alex Bealer (Barre, Mass.: Barre Publications, 1978).

CHAPTER 3 65 (bottom left) c. 1675, SPNEA. 66 Eleazer Arnold House, Lincoln, R.I., c. 1687, SPNEA. 67 (bottom) based on research by William McMillen. 68 Lynnhaven, Virginia Beach, Va., 1725. 70–71 (top) Bond Castle, Calvert County, Md., c. 1650; (bottom left) Fairfield, Carter's Creek, Va., 1692. 73 (top left) door, White-Ellery House, Gloucester, Mass.; (center) door, Corwin House, Salem, Mass., c. 1675; (bottom right) window, Plymouth County, Mass., c. 1650; all adapted from *The Framed Houses of Massachusetts Bay* by Abbot Lowell Cummings (Cambridge, Mass.: Belknap Press of Harvard University Press, 1979). (top right) door, Salem, Mass., c. 1650–1700; (bottom left) window, Barnstable, Mass., c. 1700–30; both adapted from *New England Begins* (Boston: Museum of Fine Arts, 1982). (center left) window, Buttolph-Williams House, Weathersfield, Ct., c. 1693. 74 Sparrow-Leach House, Plymouth, Mass., c. 1679, adapted from drawings (Robert St. George & Robert Trent) in *New England Begins*. 75 Cushing Barn, Hingham, Mass., c. 1695, adapted from drawings (Robert St. George & Robert F. Trent) in *Common Places*, ed. Dell Upton & John Michael Vlach (Athens, Ga.: University of Georgia Press, 1986).

CHAPTER 4 77 Meason House, Philadelphia, 1802, adapted from measured drawings (Raymond Celli) in *The Early Architecture of Western Pennsylvania* by Charles Stotz (New York: W. Helburn, 1936). 78–79 Blandfield, Tappahannock, Va., 1769–73, HABS. 81 Gadsden House, Charleston, S.C., 1800, HABS. 82, 85 (top left), 87 (top left), 89 (bottom), Cowles House, Farmington, Ct., 1761, adapted from *Great Georgian Houses of America*, vol. 1 (New York: Kalkhoff Press, 1933). 83 (top) adapted from *Early Domestic Architecture of Connecticut* by J. Frederick Kelly (New York: Dover Publications, 1963). 84 (top) Deane-Barstow House, East Taunton, Mass., c. 1800, AIA (Kenneth Clark); (bottom) Roberts House, Washington County, Pa., adapted from measured drawings (C. A. McGrill) in *The Early Architecture of Western Pennsylvania*. 85 (top right) John Imlay House, Allentown, N.J., c. 1792, AIA (Kenneth Clark). 87 (top right) AIA. 88 (bottom right) John Stuart House, Charleston, S.C., c. 1770, adapted from measured drawings (H. J. Pringle) in *Great Georgian Houses of America*; (bottom left) Colross House, Alexandria, Va., 1799, AIA (Kenneth Clark). 89 (top) AIA (Kenneth Clark); (center) Beverly, Pocomoke River, Md., AIA.

CHAPTER 5 91 William Waln House, Philadelphia, 1805–8, arch. Benjamin Henry Latrobe. 92 (bottom left) plan, Harrison Gray Otis House, Boston, 1806, arch. Charles Bulfinch, adapted from *The American Heritage History of Notable American Houses* by Marshall Davidson (New York: American Heritage Publishing, 1971). 93 (top) Brewton-Sawter House, Charleston, S.C., AIA (Kenneth Clark);

(bottom) Thomas Bennet House, AIA (A. T. S. Stoney); 94 No. 55 Beacon Street, Boston, 1807, AIA (Kenneth Clark). 95 (top) William Blacklock House, Charleston, S.C., c. 1800; (bottom) Mount Nebo, Baldwin County, Ga., HABS (J. B. Richardson). 96 Smith House, Wiscasset, Me., c. 1792, AIA (Kenneth Clark). 97 Vreeland House, Nordhoff, N.J., 1818, AIA (Kenneth Clark). 99 (top) door, Rose Hill, Lexington, Ky., HABS; (center) door, Charleston, S.C., AIA (Kenneth Clark). 100 Brevoort House, N.Y.C., 1834, attributed to archs. Ithiel Town & A. J. Davis. 101 (top) Joseph Bowers House, Northampton, Mass., c. 1830, arch. Ithiel Town; (bottom) interior, Gordon-Banks House, Ga., adapted from *The Architecture of Georgia* by Frederick Nichols (Savannah: Beehive Press, 1976). 102 (top) Rattle and Snap, Columbia, Tenn., 1845; (bottom left) plan, adapted from *Greek Revival Architecture in America* by Talbot Hamlin (New York: Oxford University Press, 1944); (bottom right) fireplace adapted from *The Architect, or Practical House Carpenter* by Asher Benjamin (New York: Dover Publications, 1988; reprint of 1830 ed.). 103 (top) Rutledge House, Troup County, Ga., 1852; (bottom) fireplace adapted from *The Beauties of Modern Architecture* by Minard Lafever (New York: Da Capo Press, 1968; reprint of 3rd ed. [New York: D. Appleton, 1839]). 104 based on Le Petit Salon, Vieux Carré, New Orleans, 1838. 105 (top right) door, Hendrix House, Riceville, Pa., adapted from photos and measured drawings (Robert Schmertz) in *The Early Architecture of Western Pennsylvania* by Charles Stotz (New York: W. Helburn, 1936); (bottom left) door, Diamond Point, Harrodsburg, Ky., adapted from *Old Kentucky Architecture* by Rexford Newcomb (New York: W. Helburn, 1940); (bottom right) door, Curtis-Devon House, Mt. Vernon, Ohio, HABS (R. W. Frend & H. C. Summersett). 106 (top) Dunton House, Belvidere, Ill., HABS (Bertha Whitman); (bottom) Starr Street House, New London, Ct., 1825. 107 Alsop House, Middletown, Ct., 1838, adapted from *Great Georgian Houses of America*, vol. 2 (New York: Kalkhoff Press, 1933).

CHAPTER 6 109 Poole Cottage, Gloucester, Mass., AIA (Frank Brown). 110–11 Sawyer-Blackwell Farm, Sweden, Me., adapted from *Big House, Little House, Back House, Barn* by Thomas Hubka (Hanover, N.H.: University Press of New England, 1984). 112 Whiddon Cabin, Forest Capital Museum, Perry, Fla.; (bottom) adapted from *Classic Cracker* by Ronald Haase (Sarasota, Fla.: Pineapple Press, 1992). 113 adapted from *Classic Cracker*. 114–15 adapted from *New Orleans Architecture* (Gretna, La.: Pelican Publishing, 1974). 118 (top, bottom) adapted from photos in *True Sod* by Barbara Oringderff (North Neton, Kans.: Mennonite Press, 1976). 120 David Crenshaw House, Fayette County, Ky., adapted from *Antebellum Architecture of Kentucky* by Clay Lancaster (Lexington: University Press of Kentucky, 1991); 121 John Bowman II House, Mercer County, Ky., adapted from *Antebellum Architecture of Kentucky*; 124 Krause House, Kirchhayne, Wis. 125 Klein-Naegelin House, New Braunfels, Tex., c. 1846, HABS (Richard Werner & Glen Wilson). 126 Long S Box and Strip House, Martin County, Tex., HABS (Joseph Ruscin). 128–29 Estudillo House, San Diego, c. 1825, HABS (Richard Wilkinson). 130 Guadalupe Rancho Adobe, Guadalupe, Cal., HABS (Arthur Fox). 131 Larkin House, Monterey, Cal., c. 1840, HABS (Richard Berteaux). 132 Trescony Barn, Rancho San Lucas, Cal., adapted from photos (Morley Baer) in *Adobes in the Sun* by Augusta Fink (San Francisco: Chronicle Books, 1972). 133 adapted from photos in *New Mexico Style* by Nancy Hunter Warren (Santa Fe: Museum of New Mexico Press, 1986).

CHAPTER 7   136 Belmead, Powhatan County, Va., c. 1845, arch. A. J. Davis. 137 (bottom) Lyndhurst, Tarrytown, N.Y., 1838, arch. A. J. Davis., NTHP. 138 Bowen House, Woodstock, Ct., 1846, arch. Joseph Wells, SPNEA. 139 Wayside Cottage, adapted from *Sloan's Victorian Houses* by Samuel Sloan (New York: Dover Publications, 1980; reprint of *The Model Architect* [Philadelphia: E. S. Jones, 1852]). 140 *Sloan's Victorian Houses.* 141 (top left, center) adapted from *The Architecture of Country Houses* by A. J. Downing (New York: Dover Publications, 1969; reprint of 1850 edition [New York: D. Appleton]); (bottom right) Green-Meldrim House, Savannah, c. 1850. 142–44 adapted from *Sloan's Victorian Houses.* 146 Benjamin Petty House, Clayton, Ala., c. 1860, HABS (Waid, Holmes & Assoc.). 147 adapted from *The American Agriculturalist*, 1885; in *The Old House Book of Barns* by Richard Rawson (New York: Sterling Publishing, 1990). 148–49 John Anderton House and Stable, Chicopee Falls, Mass., c. 1879. 150, 152 Seabright, N.J., house, c. 1875, arch. R. H. Robertson. 153 Samuel Pratt House, Newport, R.I., c. 1872; plan (Warren Oakley) adapted from *The Architectural Heritage of Newport, Rhode Island* by Antoinette Downing & Vincent Scully, Jr. (New York: American Legacy Press, 1982). 154, 156 San Francisco house, adapted from photos (Morley Baer) in *Painted Ladies* by Elizabeth Pomada & Michael Larsen (New York: E. P. Dutton, 1978). 155 Smythe House, Washington, D.C., c. 1883, arch. W. Claude Frederic. 157 c. 1875, archs. A. Kimbel & J. Cabus. 158 Short Hills, N.J., house, c. 1880, archs. Lamb & Wheeler, adapted from *Victorian Domestic Architectural Plans and Details* by William T. Comstock (New York: Dover Publications, 1987; reprint of *Modern Architectural Designs and Detail* [New York: Architectural Publisher, 1881]). 159 Eldridge Johnson House, 1882, Cape May, N.J., HABS (Benson). 161 (bottom), 162 adapted from *George F. Barber's Cottage Souvenir Number Two* by George F. Barber (Watkins Glen, N.Y.: American Life, 1982). 163 Short Hills, N.J., house, c. 1882, archs. Lamb & Rich. 164 Dudley House, Waverly, Mass., 1908, arch. William Northrup. 163 (top) L. W. Bacon House, Norwich, Ct., 1882, arch. Stephen Farle; (bottom) Williams Stable, Cohassett, Mass., c. 1901, arch. J. A. Schweinfurth. 166–67 Carroll Street houses, Brooklyn, 1888, arch. C. P. H. Gilbert, adapted from measured drawing (Robert Hartman & Harry Hansen) in *Guide to New York City Landmarks* by New York City Landmarks Preservation Commission (Washington, D.C.: Preservation Press., 1992). 168 Sylvester Everett House, Cleveland, 1883, arch. Charles Schweinfurth, adapted from *American Country Houses of the Gilded Age* by Arnold Lewis (New York: Dover Publications, 1982; reprint of George William Sheldon's *Artistic Country-Seats* [New York: D. Appleton, 1886–87]). 169 Sturtevant Stable, Brookline, Mass., c. 1901, arch. W. G. Preston. 170–71 Read Lodge, Adirondacks, N.Y., 1905, archs. Davis, McGrath & Sherwood. 172 Courtesy Adirondack Museum, Blue Mountain Lake, N.Y. 173 Edward Mallinckrodt Boathouse, arch. Augustus Shephard. 174 1889, arch. William S. Wicks. 175 (bottom left) Grace Church Rectory, N.Y.C., c. 1845, adapted from photo (Robert Mayer) in *Bricks and Brownstone: The New York Row House, 1783–1929* by Charles Lockwood (New York: McGraw-Hill, 1972); (bottom right) Wheelwright House, Woods Hole, Mass., 1888.

CHAPTER 8   177 (bottom) Biltmore, Asheville, N.C., 1895, arch. Richard Morris Hunt. 178 Burrage House, Boston, 1899, arch. Charles Brigham. 179 H. A. C. Taylor House, N.Y.C., 1896, archs. McKim, Mead & White., adapted from *A Monograph of the Works of McKim, Mead & White, 1879–1915* (New York:

Da Capo Press, 1985; reprint of 1925 ed. [New York: Architectural Book Publishing]). 180 Pulitzer House, N.Y.C., 1903, archs. McKim, Mead & White, adapted from *A Monograph of the Works of McKim, Mead & White.* 182 (top) Charles Garret House, Norristown, Pa., 1913, arch. Gordon McCririe; (bottom) archs. Taylor & Levi; both adapted from *House and Garden's Book of Houses* (New York: Condé Nast, 1920). 183 4 East 74th St., N.Y.C., 1900, arch. Alexander Welch. 184 The Elms, Newport, R.I., 1901, arch. Horace Trumbauer. 185 J. R. De Lamar House, N.Y.C., 1903, arch. C. P. H. Gilbert. 186–87 William Evans House, Greenwich, Ct., archs. J. E. R. Carpenter & Walter D. Blair Assoc. 188 Arthur Keith House, Washington Heights, D.C., 1899, arch. Waddy B. Wood. 189 (top, bottom left) Andrew Stout House, Redbank, N.J., arch. John Russell Pope. 190–91 (top) Frederick Coffin House, Brookline, Mass., 1900, arch. J. A. Sceweinfurth. 191 (bottom) Marshall Morgan House, Philadelphia, 1912, archs. Thomas, Churchman & Molitor. 192 (top, center) Lathrop Brown House, St. James, N.Y., 1922, arch. Peabody, Wilson & Brown; (bottom) George Herron House, Portland, Ore., arch. Harold Doty, adapted from *Architectural Record*, Feb. 1927. 193 (top) adapted from *House Beautiful*, Feb. 1920; (bottom) Frenaye House, Llewellyn Park, N.J., 1935, archs. Howard & Frenaye. 194 Gambrill House, Newport, R.I., archs. Carrere & Hastings. 195 Weston Stable, Dalton, Mass., 1902, arch. J. Vance. 196 George Washington Smith House, Santa Barbara, Cal., c. 1899, arch. George Washington Smith. 197 (top) Edward Hosmer House, Pasadena, Cal., 1986, archs. Greene & Greene, adapted from *Greene and Greene* by Randell Makinson (Salt Lake City: Peregrine Smith, 1979); (bottom) Lewis Garage, Racine, Wis., archs. Guilbert & Funston. 198 (left) George Washington Smith House; (top right) desn. Samuel Yellin; hinges, der. P. A. Fiebiger; all adapted from *Spanish Influence on American Architecture and Decoration* by R. W. Sexton (New York: Brentano's, 1927). 199 "El Fureidis," 1903, arch. Bertram Goodhue. 200 (top) Brookline, Mass., house, 1912, archs. Allen & Collens; (bottom) garage, arch. Bernhardt Muller, adapted from *Pencil Points*, March 1936. 201 Edith Bogue House, Montclair, N.J., arch. Clifford Wendehack, adapted from *Architectural Record*, Feb. 1924.

CHAPTER 9   203 arch. Frank Lloyd Wright, adapted from *Drawings and Plans of Frank Lloyd Wright* (New York: Dover Publications, 1983). 204–5 Susan Lawrence Dana House, Springfield, Ill. (Dana-Thomas House State Historic Site), 1902–4, arch. Frank Lloyd Wright, HABS (James Hollis). 206 (top) Frank Hall House, Oak Park, Ill., 1904, arch. Eben Roberts. 207 (top) Avery Coonley House, Riverside, Ill., 1908, arch. Frank Lloyd Wright, adapted from *Drawings and Plans of Frank Lloyd Wright*; (bottom center) Amberg House, Grand Rapids, Mich., 1913, arch. R. V. Von Holst; (bottom right) Dana-Thomas House. 208–9 Theodore M. Irwin House, Pasadena, Cal., 1906, archs. Greene & Greene, HABS. 209 (bottom) plan adapted from *The American Bungalow* by Clay Lancaster (New York: Abbeville Press, 1985). 210 (top) garage, James A. Culberson House, Pasadena, Cal., 1906; (bottom left), door, Mary E. Cole House, Pasadena, 1907; (bottom center, right) Charles Sumner Greene House, Pasadena, 1901; all, archs. Greene & Greene. 211 (top) Blacker House; Pasadena, Cal., 1907, archs. Greene & Greene. 212 "Very Popular 4-Bedroom Bungalow," adapted from *117 House Designs of the Twenties* (New York: Dover Publications, 1992; reprint of *Gordon-Van Tine Homes* [Davenport, Ill.: Gordon-Van Tine, 1923]). 213 "Homelike Cottage," 1905, des. Gustav Stickley. 214, 216 adapted from *500 Small Houses of the Twenties* (New York: Dover

Publications, 1990; reprint of *The Books of a Thousand Homes*, vol. 1 ([New York: Home Owners Service Institute, 1923]). 215 adapted from *American Architect*, May 1926. 217 adapted from *The Swiss Chalet in America* by Fritz Ehrsam (Reading, Pa., 1916). 218 "The Natco Double House," arch. George Frech. 220 (top) des. Gustav Stickley, 1903; (bottom) "Modern Home Interiors," National Lumber Manufacturers Association, 1929. 221 (top left, top right, bottom right) adapted from "The Door Beautiful," Morgan Co., Oshkosh, Wis., 1911; (bottom left) des. Gustav Stickley.

CHAPTER 10   223 adapted from design by arch. Arne Kartwold, Berkeley, Cal., in *Architectural Forum*, April 1935. 225 (top) adapted from "Demonstration House for Yonkers Better Housing Committee," in *Architectural Forum*, June 1935; (bottom) adapted from design by Charles Porter, in *Architectural Forum*, April 1935. 229 Bennati House, Lake Arrowhead, Cal., 1934, arch. Rudolph Schindler, adapted from *Five California Architects* by Esther McCoy (New York: Reinhold Publishing, 1961).

CHAPTER 11   231 based on "The Palace," Travel Coach Corp., Flint, Mich., 1943. 232 adapted from "Victory House," in *Architectural Forum*, April 1943. 233 based on Dymaxion II, c. 1941, arch. R. Buckminster Fuller. 235 adapted from *The Small Homes Annual* (Washington, D.C.: Home-builders' Research Institute, 1945). 238 (bottom left) fireplace, arch. Arthur Deam; (bottom right) fireplace, archs. Leinweber, Yamasaki, & Helmuth; both adapted from *Selected Houses from PA* (New York: Reinhold Publishing, n.d.). 239 adapted from *Living on the Level* by Royal Barry Wills (Cambridge, Mass.: Houghton Mifflin, 1954). 241 based on "The Alpine," 1946, American Plan Service, Miami, Fla. 243 adapted from *More Houses for Good Living* by Royal Barry Wills (New York: Architectural Book Publishing, 1968). 245 arch. Aymar Embury, adapted from *Life Houses*, 1938. 249 Hobe Sound, Fla., house, 1956, arch. Eliot Noyes, adapted from *Twenty-five Years of Record Houses* (New York: McGraw-Hill, 1981). 250–51 Minnesota Housing Agency Demonstration House, Camden State Park, Minn., 1980, arch. Peter Pfister, adapted from *Earth-Sheltered Homes* by Donna Ahrens et al. (New York: Van Nostrand Reinhold, 1981).

CHAPTER 12   253 based on Gwathmey Residence, Amagansett, N.Y., 1966–67, arch. Charles Gwathmey. 254–55 (top) based on design by arch. Paul Rudolph, 1963. 256 based on design by arch. Bob Giddings, adapted from *The Compact House Book*, ed. Don Metz (Pownal, Vt.: Garden Way Publishing, 1983). 258 (top) based on design by archs. Willis Mills, Jr., & Timothy Martin, 1971, adapted from *Twenty-five Years of Record Houses* (New York: McGraw-Hill, 1981). 259 based on Coxe-Hayden House, Block Island, R.I., 1981, archs. Venturi, Scott Brown & Assoc. 260 based on Reid House, Johns Island, S.C., 1987, archs. Clark & Menefee. 261 Cooper House, Seaside, Fla., based on design by Don & Libby Cooper, archs. Cooper Johnson Smith. 262 based on designs by arch. Wayne Berg. 263 (top) based on designs by Huck Snyder; (bottom) based on design by arch. Mike Jackson.

Index